C# IN THE REAL WORLD

Learn to Build Robust Enterprise Applications

THOMPSON CARTER

Table of Content

TABLE OF CONTENTS

INTRODUCTION
C# IN THE REAL WORLD

In today's fast-paced world, technology continues to evolve at an unprecedented rate, and so does the demand for skilled developers who can adapt to and harness these changes. **"C# in the Real World: Learn to Build Robust Enterprise Applications"** is designed for developers who wish to master C# and take their skills from beginner to expert, while focusing on the practical, real-world applications of the language.

Whether you're just starting your programming journey or are an experienced developer looking to refine your skills, this book provides a comprehensive, hands-on guide to building scalable, maintainable, and efficient applications using C#. From learning the basics to tackling complex enterprise-level scenarios, we explore the full spectrum of C# features and their real-world applications.

The Power of C# in Modern Development

C# is a versatile, powerful language that has become a go-to choice for developers across many domains. From building desktop applications to cloud-based solutions, enterprise systems, and mobile apps, C# offers a robust platform with rich features that can be leveraged for almost any kind of development.

Throughout this book, we will explore **C#'s modern features**, such as **records**, **pattern matching**, **async programming**, and **nullability**, and see how they help developers write more expressive, maintainable, and efficient code. But this book is not just about learning syntax or understanding concepts—it's about **real-world application**.

We will dive into practical scenarios, demonstrating how to implement these advanced features in ways that address the challenges developers face when building large-scale, high-performance systems. You'll gain insight into how C# fits within modern development pipelines, including how to leverage tools like **CI/CD**, **monitoring**, and **logging** to ensure your applications run smoothly in production.

Why This Book?

1. **Clear, Actionable Content**: Each chapter is crafted to help you achieve practical results. Rather than overwhelming you with theoretical concepts, we focus on actionable lessons that you can apply immediately to real-world projects. You'll not only learn new features of C#, but also how to make your applications more scalable, efficient, and maintainable.

2. **Hands-On Examples**: The book provides step-by-step examples and case studies, such as building a **payment processing system** or optimizing a **large-scale data processing application**. These examples reflect the kinds of challenges you'll encounter in the field and show you how to solve them effectively using C#.

3. **Modern Best Practices**: In addition to learning how to use C# effectively, this book emphasizes **best practices** for software development, including **clean code, design patterns, unit testing**, and **continuous integration/delivery (CI/CD)**. These best practices will help you write code that is not only functional but also robust, maintainable, and scalable in the long term.

4. **Real-World Focus**: This book is designed for **professional developers** and aspiring experts who want to master C# in the context of **enterprise-level applications**. Each chapter includes examples that reflect the challenges faced by companies when building and maintaining software that serves thousands or even millions of users.

What You'll Learn

By the end of this book, you will:

- **Master the fundamentals and advanced features of C#**: Learn how to use C# features like **LINQ, async/await, dependency injection**, and **records** in a real-world context.
- **Write clean, maintainable, and performant code**: Understand how to apply **SOLID principles**, use **design patterns**, and follow **best practices** to ensure your code stands the test of time.
- **Build robust enterprise applications**: From small business tools to large-scale systems, you'll gain the skills to develop applications that meet enterprise demands.

- **Implement CI/CD pipelines**: Automate your build, test, and deployment processes to ensure fast and reliable delivery of software.
- **Monitor and optimize applications**: Learn how to monitor your application in production, detect and resolve performance bottlenecks, and implement **logging** and **monitoring** solutions using tools like **Serilog**, **NLog**, and **Application Insights**.
- **Prepare for the future of C#**: Stay ahead of the curve by learning about the latest features and practices, ensuring that your codebase is future-proof and ready for new technologies.

Who Should Read This Book?

This book is intended for a wide audience:

- **Beginners** who are familiar with programming concepts and wish to learn C# in the context of real-world software development.
- **Intermediate developers** who want to expand their knowledge of C# and learn how to apply modern features in practical ways.
- **Advanced developers** who are interested in mastering **enterprise-level development** with C# and learning the best practices that will help them build high-performance, maintainable systems.
- **Software engineers** who are transitioning to C# from other programming languages and want to leverage C#'s power to solve real-world challenges.

How to Use This Book

This book is designed to be both **instructional** and **hands-on**, with each chapter building on the previous one. While you can read it from start to finish, you can also focus on specific chapters based on your needs.

Each chapter contains:

- **Introduction and theory**: Provides a solid understanding of the topic, including why it matters and how it fits into the larger picture of enterprise software development.
- **Practical examples**: Walk-throughs of real-world scenarios that demonstrate how to apply the concepts to solve specific problems.
- **Exercises and challenges**: Test your knowledge and skills with exercises designed to reinforce the material and help you think critically about how to apply it in your own projects.

Chapter Closing

"C# in the Real World" is not just a book about learning a programming language; it's a comprehensive guide to using C# to build robust, scalable, and maintainable enterprise applications. Whether you're developing small business apps, large-scale systems, or cloud-based solutions, the tools, techniques, and best practices in this book will help you write efficient, high-quality software.

By the end of this journey, you will not only be proficient in C# but also equipped with the knowledge and practices to tackle real-world software development challenges. So, let's get started and prepare to build the future of C# applications!

CHAPTER ONE

Introduction to C# and Enterprise Applications

Overview of C#: History, Syntax, and Modern Features

History of C#:

- C# was developed by Microsoft in the early 2000s under the leadership of Anders Hejlsberg, a prominent figure in software development. Its first release was in 2002, as part of the .NET framework.
- Designed to be simple, modern, and robust, C# aimed to combine the power of C++ with the simplicity of Java, offering developers a better experience for building Windows applications.
- Over time, C# has evolved significantly, with each new version introducing modern features to meet the needs of developers working with new technologies like cloud computing, web development, and machine learning.

Syntax Overview:

- C# is an object-oriented language, meaning everything is treated as an object, which encapsulates both data and methods.
- It uses a syntax similar to C, C++, and Java, making it easier for developers familiar with those languages to learn C#.
- Basic structure:
  - **Variables**: `int age = 30;`, `string name = "John";`

- o **Methods**: `public void Greet() { Console.WriteLine("Hello"); }`
- o **Control flow**: `if (x > y) { ... } else { ... }`
- o **Classes and Objects**: `class Person { public string Name; }`

Modern Features of C#:

- **LINQ (Language Integrated Query)**: A powerful feature for querying collections in a declarative way. With LINQ, developers can query data from arrays, databases, and XML files using a SQL-like syntax directly in C#.
- **Asynchronous Programming**: C# introduced the `async` and `await` keywords, allowing developers to write asynchronous code that's clean and easy to follow, enabling better performance in I/O-bound operations.
- **Pattern Matching**: C# 7.0 introduced pattern matching, simplifying complex conditional logic and allowing for cleaner, more readable code.
- **Nullable Reference Types**: C# 8.0 brought nullable reference types, helping developers write safer code by making it clear when variables can be `null`.
- **Records and Immutable Types**: Introduced in C# 9.0, records are a new type of class that makes it easier to create immutable data objects. They provide built-in functionality like value-based equality comparisons.

Why C# for Enterprise Development?

1. Versatility and Cross-Platform Support:

- C# is widely used for both desktop and web development through frameworks like WPF (Windows Presentation Foundation) and ASP.NET Core.

- With .NET Core, developers can now build cross-platform applications that run on Windows, Linux, and macOS, increasing C#'s appeal for enterprise solutions beyond just Windows environments.

2. Scalability and Performance:

- C# has performance benefits due to its close integration with the .NET runtime and its ability to handle both small and large-scale applications efficiently.
- Memory management and garbage collection ensure applications are optimized for better performance, crucial for handling high-traffic enterprise systems.

3. Robust Ecosystem:

- The .NET ecosystem offers a wide range of libraries, tools, and services that integrate seamlessly with C#, allowing developers to implement everything from simple web applications to complex enterprise solutions.
- C# works well with other Microsoft technologies like Azure, SQL Server, and Active Directory, which are often used in enterprise settings.

4. Strong Typing and Safety:

- C#'s strong typing and compile-time checking ensure fewer runtime errors, which are crucial for enterprise applications that handle sensitive data and require high reliability.
- Features like exception handling, nullable reference types, and immutable types contribute to safer and more maintainable code.

5. Security Features:

- C# supports strong security features like code access security, type safety, and built-in encryption libraries, making it an excellent choice for enterprise applications where data integrity and security are paramount.

Real-World Use Cases: Examples of C# in Large-Scale Projects

1. Microsoft Enterprise Solutions:

- Microsoft itself uses C# extensively in its internal and customer-facing enterprise applications. Examples include Microsoft Office (especially with Office 365), Dynamics 365 (business applications), and even the backend systems powering Azure.

2. E-Commerce Platforms:

- Major e-commerce platforms such as eBay and Alibaba utilize C# in their enterprise backend systems to handle millions of transactions per day with a focus on scalability and speed.

3. Financial Services:

- Many large banks and financial institutions use C# for developing trading platforms, risk management systems, and financial analysis tools. C#'s performance and stability make it ideal for applications that require precise and secure real-time transactions.

4. Healthcare Systems:

- Healthcare organizations use C# to build applications for managing patient records, appointment scheduling, and billing. The language's security features ensure that sensitive health data is handled according to regulatory standards like HIPAA.

5. Logistics and Supply Chain Management:

- C# is also employed in building complex enterprise software for logistics and supply chain management, where real-time tracking, inventory management, and reporting systems require high efficiency and scalability.

Getting Started: Setting Up Your Development Environment (IDE, Tools)

1. Choosing an Integrated Development Environment (IDE):

- **Visual Studio**: The most popular and powerful IDE for C# development. It offers full integration with the .NET ecosystem, including features like IntelliSense (code suggestions), debugging, and project templates for web, desktop, and cloud-based applications.
  - o Download Visual Studio from here.
- **Visual Studio Code**: A lighter, cross-platform alternative for developers who prefer a more flexible environment. Visual Studio Code is an excellent choice for C# development with the appropriate extensions.
  - o Install Visual Studio Code from here.

2. Installing .NET SDK:

- To run C# applications, you need to install the .NET SDK (Software Development Kit), which includes the tools needed for building and running applications.
  - o Download the .NET SDK from here.

3. Setting Up the Development Environment:

- After installing Visual Studio or Visual Studio Code, you'll need to set up the .NET framework. Follow the setup instructions for creating a new console application, web app, or any other type of project.
- For web development with ASP.NET Core, you can create projects using predefined templates in Visual Studio or through the command line using the `dotnet` CLI.

4. Running Your First C# Program:

- Once you've installed the tools, open Visual Studio, create a new project, and select a C# template (like a console application). Write your first "Hello World" program:

```csharp
Copy
using System;

class Program
{
    static void Main(string[] args)
    {
        Console.WriteLine("Hello,
World!");
    }
}
```

- Run the application to see your first C# program in action!

This chapter sets the stage for deeper exploration into C# and enterprise-level development. It introduces key concepts about C# and its power for building scalable, maintainable, and secure applications, while guiding readers through the tools and environment they'll need to start coding. Would you like any adjustments or more details on any part?

CHAPTER TWO

Understanding Object-Oriented Programming (OOP) in C#

Principles of OOP: Classes, Objects, Inheritance, Polymorphism, Encapsulation, and Abstraction

Object-Oriented Programming (OOP) is a programming paradigm that organizes software design around data, or objects, rather than functions and logic. Objects are instances of classes, and each object can hold data and methods. C# is fundamentally object-oriented, making it crucial to understand its core principles.

1. Classes and Objects

- **Class**: A class is a blueprint or template for creating objects. It defines the properties (data) and methods (behavior) that an object created from the class will have.

```
csharp
Copy
public class Product
{
    public string Name { get; set; }
    public decimal Price { get; set; }

    public void DisplayProductInfo()
    {
        Console.WriteLine($"Product:
{Name}, Price: {Price}");
```

```
    }
}
```

- **Object**: An object is an instance of a class. When you create an object, you're creating an instance of that class, with its own data and behavior.

```csharp
csharp
Copy
Product product = new Product();
product.Name = "Laptop";
product.Price = 1200.99M;
product.DisplayProductInfo();   // Output:
Product: Laptop, Price: 1200.99
```

2. Inheritance

- **Inheritance** allows one class to inherit the properties and methods of another. This helps to reuse code and create a hierarchy between classes.

```csharp
csharp
Copy
public class Electronics : Product
{
    public string Brand { get; set; }

    public void DisplayBrandInfo()
    {
        Console.WriteLine($"Brand:
{Brand}");
    }
}

Electronics laptop = new Electronics();
laptop.Name = "Laptop";
laptop.Price = 1200.99M;
laptop.Brand = "Dell";
laptop.DisplayProductInfo();  // Inherited
from Product
```

```
laptop.DisplayBrandInfo();        // Output:
Brand: Dell
```

- In this example, the `Electronics` class inherits the properties and methods from the `Product` class, making it easy to extend or customize the `Product` class without rewriting code.

3. Polymorphism

- **Polymorphism** allows objects of different classes to be treated as objects of a common base class. It also refers to the ability of methods to behave differently based on the object they are acting upon.
- **Method Overriding**: A subclass can provide a specific implementation of a method that is already defined in its base class.

```csharp
csharp
Copy
public class Product
{
    public virtual void DisplayInfo()
    {
        Console.WriteLine("Product
information.");
    }
}

public class Electronics : Product
{
    public override void DisplayInfo()
    {
        Console.WriteLine("Electronics
product information.");
    }
}

Product product = new Electronics();
```

```
product.DisplayInfo();        //    Output:
Electronics product information.
```

- **Method Overloading**: C# allows the same method to have different signatures (i.e., varying parameters), making it easier to reuse method names.

```csharp
Copy
public class Product
{
    public void DisplayInfo(string name)
    {
        Console.WriteLine($"Product:
{name}");
    }

    public void DisplayInfo(string name,
decimal price)
    {
        Console.WriteLine($"Product:
{name}, Price: {price}");
    }
}
```

4. Encapsulation

- **Encapsulation** refers to the practice of hiding the internal state of an object and only exposing methods that interact with that state. This helps prevent unintended changes to an object's data and allows the internal implementation to be modified without affecting other parts of the code.

```csharp
Copy
public class Product
{
    private decimal price;

    public decimal Price
```

```
        {
                get { return price; }
                set
                {
                    if (value >= 0)
                        price = value;
                    else
                        Console.WriteLine("Price
        cannot be negative.");
                }
            }
        }

        Product product = new Product();
        product.Price = 1500;
        Console.WriteLine(product.Price);      //
        Output: 1500
        product.Price = -50;   // Output:  Price
        cannot be negative.
```

- Here, the `Price` property is encapsulated, and the setter ensures that no negative values can be assigned.

5. Abstraction

- **Abstraction** is the concept of hiding complex implementation details and showing only the essential features of an object. This can be done through abstract classes or interfaces.
- **Abstract Class**: An abstract class cannot be instantiated directly and can contain abstract methods that must be implemented in derived classes.

```
csharp
Copy
public abstract class Product
{
```

```
        public abstract void DisplayInfo();
}

public class Electronics : Product
{
    public override void DisplayInfo()
    {
        Console.WriteLine("Electronics
Product Info.");
    }
}
```

- **Interface**: An interface defines a contract that classes can implement, specifying which methods must be implemented but leaving the details to the classes.

```
csharp
Copy
public interface IProduct
{
    void DisplayInfo();
}

public class Electronics : IProduct
{
    public void DisplayInfo()
    {
        Console.WriteLine("Electronics
Product Info.");
    }
}
```

Real-World Example: Building a Simple OOP-Based Inventory System

Let's build a small inventory system for a store that handles different types of products like electronics and clothing. We'll use the core principles of OOP to organize the system.

Step 1: Define the Base Class

We start by defining the `Product` class, which will be the base class for all product types.

```csharp
Copy
public class Product
{
    public string Name { get; set; }
    public decimal Price { get; set; }

    public virtual void DisplayInfo()
    {
        Console.WriteLine($"Product:     {Name}, Price: {Price}");
    }
}
```

Step 2: Create Derived Classes

We then create specialized classes for specific product types. In this case, we'll have `Electronics` and `Clothing` classes that inherit from `Product`.

```csharp
Copy
public class Electronics : Product
{
    public string Brand { get; set; }

    public override void DisplayInfo()
    {
        Console.WriteLine($"Electronics - Brand: {Brand}, Name: {Name}, Price: {Price}");
    }
}

public class Clothing : Product
{
    public string Size { get; set; }
```

```
    public override void DisplayInfo()
    {
        Console.WriteLine($"Clothing   -   Size:
{Size}, Name: {Name}, Price: {Price}");
    }
}
```

Step 3: Use the Classes in the Inventory System

Now, let's create an inventory system to manage the products.

```csharp
Copy
public class Inventory
{
    private List<Product> products = new
List<Product>();

    public void AddProduct(Product product)
    {
        products.Add(product);
    }

    public void DisplayInventory()
    {
        foreach (var product in products)
        {
            product.DisplayInfo();
        }
    }
}
```

Step 4: Testing the System

Finally, we'll add some products to the inventory and display them.

```csharp
Copy
class Program
```

```
{
    static void Main()
    {
        var inventory = new Inventory();

        var laptop = new Electronics { Name =
"Laptop", Price = 1200.99M, Brand = "Dell" };
        var shirt = new Clothing { Name =
"Shirt", Price = 25.99M, Size = "L" };

        inventory.AddProduct(laptop);
        inventory.AddProduct(shirt);

        inventory.DisplayInventory();
    }
}
```

Output:

```yaml
yaml
Copy
Electronics - Brand: Dell, Name: Laptop, Price:
1200.99
Clothing - Size: L, Name: Shirt, Price: 25.99
```

Best Practices: Writing Clean, Reusable Code

1. **Use Meaningful Names**: Choose clear and descriptive names for classes, methods, and variables to make the code self-explanatory.
2. **Keep Methods Short**: A method should do one thing and do it well. This makes it easier to understand, test, and maintain.
3. **Avoid Duplication**: Use inheritance and composition to avoid code repetition. Create reusable components where possible.
4. **Encapsulate Properly**: Keep the internal state of objects private, and provide public methods to

C# IN THE REAL WORLD

interact with them safely. Avoid exposing implementation details unnecessarily.

5. **Use Interfaces and Abstract Classes**: Design with interfaces and abstract classes to define clear contracts for your code. This encourages loose coupling and greater flexibility.

6. **Apply SOLID Principles**: These principles help to create code that is easy to maintain and extend:
   o Single Responsibility Principle
   o Open/Closed Principle
   o Liskov Substitution Principle
   o Interface Segregation Principle
   o Dependency Inversion Principle

This chapter introduces OOP concepts and applies them in a practical, real-world example of an inventory system. By following these principles and best practices, developers can create maintainable, scalable, and reusable code for enterprise applications. Would you like to dive deeper into any of the concepts or see more examples?

27

CHAPTER THREE

Mastering C# Data Types and Collections

Primitive Data Types: Int, Float, String, etc.

In C#, data types are divided into **primitive** types (also known as simple types) and **complex** types. Primitive types are the building blocks of any application. They define the type of data that a variable can hold, and they are essential for writing efficient and effective code.

1. Integer Types

- **int**: Represents a 32-bit signed integer.

  ```csharp
  csharp
  Copy
  int age = 30;
  ```

- **long**: Represents a 64-bit signed integer, used for larger numbers.

  ```csharp
  csharp
  Copy
  long population = 7800000000L;
  ```

2. Floating-Point Types

- **float**: Represents a single-precision floating-point number.

  ```csharp
  csharp
  ```

```
Copy
float price = 19.99F;
```

- **double**: Represents a double-precision floating-point number, suitable for higher precision.

```
csharp
Copy
double distance = 1563.75;
```

3. Boolean Type

- **bool**: Represents a boolean value (true or false).

```
csharp
Copy
bool isActive = true;
```

4. Character Type

- **char**: Represents a single 16-bit Unicode character.

```
csharp
Copy
char grade = 'A';
```

5. String Type

- **string**: Represents a sequence of characters, commonly used for text.

```
csharp
Copy
string name = "John Doe";
```

6. Special Types

- **decimal**: Represents a 128-bit precise decimal value, ideal for financial calculations.

```
csharp
Copy
```

```
decimal salary = 4500.75M;
```

- **var**: Used for implicitly typed variables where the type is inferred by the compiler based on the assigned value.

```
csharp
Copy
var age = 30;   // int type is inferred
```

Complex Data Types: Arrays, Lists, Dictionaries, and Custom Collections

Complex data types allow you to store and manipulate more sophisticated data structures. C# provides several built-in complex types that are used extensively in enterprise applications.

1. Arrays

An **array** is a fixed-size collection of elements of the same type. Arrays are useful when you need to store multiple items, but the number of items is known ahead of time.

```
csharp
Copy
int[] scores = new int[] { 90, 85, 77, 92 };
Console.WriteLine(scores[0]);   // Output: 90
```

- Arrays are zero-indexed, meaning the first element has an index of 0.

2. Lists

A **List** is a dynamic array provided by the `System.Collections.Generic` namespace. Unlike arrays, lists can grow and shrink in size dynamically.

```csharp
Copy
List<string> customers = new List<string> {
"Alice", "Bob", "Charlie" };
customers.Add("David");
Console.WriteLine(customers[2]);      // Output:
Charlie
```

- Lists are more flexible than arrays and are often used in applications where the size of the collection changes frequently.

3. Dictionaries

A **Dictionary** is a collection of key-value pairs. It allows for fast lookups based on a unique key, making it an ideal choice for mapping relationships between data.

```csharp
Copy
Dictionary<int, string> employees = new
Dictionary<int, string>();
employees.Add(1, "John Doe");
employees.Add(2, "Jane Smith");

Console.WriteLine(employees[1]);      // Output:
John Doe
```

- The keys in a dictionary must be unique, but the values can be duplicated.

4. Custom Collections

Sometimes, you may need to define your own collection types. C# allows you to create custom collections by extending existing collection types or implementing interfaces like IEnumerable.

```csharp
Copy
public class ProductCollection : ICollection<string>
{
    private List<string> products = new List<string>();

    public int Count => products.Count;

    public bool IsReadOnly => false;

    public void Add(string item)
    {
        products.Add(item);
    }

    public void Clear()
    {
        products.Clear();
    }

    public bool Contains(string item)
    {
        return products.Contains(item);
    }

    public void CopyTo(string[] array, int arrayIndex)
    {
        products.CopyTo(array, arrayIndex);
    }

    public IEnumerator<string> GetEnumerator()
```

```
    {
        return products.GetEnumerator();
    }

    public bool Remove(string item)
    {
        return products.Remove(item);
    }

    System.Collections.IEnumerator
System.Collections.IEnumerable.GetEnumerator()
    {
        return products.GetEnumerator();
    }
}
```

In this example, we've created a custom collection class `ProductCollection` that wraps around a list of strings.

Real-World Example: A Customer Management System Using Collections

Let's build a simple customer management system using collections. This example will demonstrate how to use C# data types and collections (Lists and Dictionaries) in a real-world context.

Step 1: Define the Customer Class

We'll define a `Customer` class that will represent a customer in our system.

```csharp
Copy
public class Customer
{
    public int Id { get; set; }
```

```csharp
    public string Name { get; set; }
    public string Email { get; set; }
    public DateTime DateOfBirth { get; set; }

    public Customer(int id, string name, string
email, DateTime dateOfBirth)
    {
        Id = id;
        Name = name;
        Email = email;
        DateOfBirth = dateOfBirth;
    }

    public void DisplayInfo()
    {
        Console.WriteLine($"ID:    {Id},    Name:
{Name},   Email:   {Email},   Date   of   Birth:
{DateOfBirth.ToShortDateString()}");
    }
}
```

Step 2: Create a Customer Management System

Next, we'll create a class CustomerManagementSystem that
uses a Dictionary to store customers. The Dictionary will
map customer IDs to Customer objects, allowing quick
lookups based on the customer's ID.

```csharp
csharp
Copy
public class CustomerManagementSystem
{
    private Dictionary<int, Customer> customers
= new Dictionary<int, Customer>();

    public void AddCustomer(Customer customer)
    {
        customers[customer.Id] = customer;
    }

    public Customer GetCustomer(int id)
    {
```

```csharp
        if (customers.ContainsKey(id))
        {
            return customers[id];
        }
        else
        {
            Console.WriteLine("Customer          not
found.");
            return null;
        }
    }

    public void DisplayAllCustomers()
    {
        foreach         (var         customer         in
customers.Values)
        {
            customer.DisplayInfo();
        }
    }
}
```

Step 3: Implement the Main Program

Finally, let's implement a program that uses the
CustomerManagementSystem to add and retrieve customers.

```csharp
csharp
Copy
class Program
{
    static void Main(string[] args)
    {
        var     customerSystem      =       new
CustomerManagementSystem();

        // Adding customers to the system
        var customer1 = new Customer(1,  "Alice
Johnson",        "alice@example.com",         new
DateTime(1985, 5, 12));
        var customer2 = new Customer(2,  "Bob
Smith", "bob@example.com", new DateTime(1992, 3,
25));
```

```
customerSystem.AddCustomer(customer1);
customerSystem.AddCustomer(customer2);

// Displaying all customers
Console.WriteLine("All Customers:");
customerSystem.DisplayAllCustomers();

// Retrieve and display a specific
customer
Console.WriteLine("\nRetrieving Customer
ID 1:");
var          retrievedCustomer          =
customerSystem.GetCustomer(1);
if (retrievedCustomer != null)
{
    retrievedCustomer.DisplayInfo();
}
    }
}
```

Output:

```
yaml
Copy
All Customers:
ID:   1,   Name:   Alice   Johnson,   Email:
alice@example.com, Date of Birth: 05/12/1985
ID: 2, Name: Bob Smith, Email: bob@example.com,
Date of Birth: 03/25/1992

Retrieving Customer ID 1:
ID:   1,   Name:   Alice   Johnson,   Email:
alice@example.com, Date of Birth: 05/12/1985
```

In this example, the customer data is stored in a Dictionary<int, Customer>, allowing fast retrieval of customers based on their ID. The CustomerManagementSystem class provides methods to add, retrieve, and display customer information.

Best Practices for Working with Collections

1. **Use Appropriate Collection Types**: Choose the right collection type based on your needs:
   o   Use **List<T>** for dynamic, ordered collections.
   o   Use **Dictionary<TKey, TValue>** for collections that require fast lookups by key.
   o   Use **Queue<T>** and **Stack<T>** for FIFO (first-in-first-out) and LIFO (last-in-first-out) operations, respectively.
2. **Avoid Overuse of Arrays**: While arrays are useful, they have a fixed size and lack many helpful features. Use `List<T>` or other dynamic collections when the size is not fixed.
3. **Minimize Memory Consumption**: When working with large datasets, consider using more memory-efficient collections or techniques, such as lazy loading or streams.
4. **Understand Collection Thread Safety**: Some collections are thread-safe (e.g., `ConcurrentDictionary`), while others are not. Make sure to choose thread-safe collections when working in multi-threaded environments.
5. **Use LINQ for Querying Collections**: LINQ allows you to query collections in a more readable and efficient way. Use LINQ methods like `Where()`, `Select()`, and `OrderBy()` to filter and sort collections.

This chapter introduced C# data types and collections, showing how they can be used to store and manipulate data in real-world applications. The customer management system demonstrated practical applications of collections, and best practices were highlighted to ensure efficient and maintainable code. Would you like to see more advanced examples or specific use cases?

CHAPTER FOUR

Control Flow and Exception Handling

Conditional Statements: if, switch, etc.

Conditional statements in C# allow you to make decisions in your code based on certain conditions. They are essential for directing the flow of execution depending on specific criteria.

1. if Statement

The `if` statement is used to execute a block of code only if a specified condition is true. You can also include an `else` block to execute code when the condition is false.

```csharp
Copy
int age = 18;

if (age >= 18)
{
    Console.WriteLine("You    are    eligible    to
vote.");
}
else
{
    Console.WriteLine("You    are    not    eligible    to
vote.");
}
```

- In this example, the condition checks if `age` is greater than or equal to 18 and prints the corresponding message.

2. else if Statement

You can use `else if` to check for multiple conditions in sequence. This allows you to test several different possibilities.

```csharp
Copy
int score = 85;

if (score >= 90)
{
    Console.WriteLine("Grade: A");
}
else if (score >= 80)
{
    Console.WriteLine("Grade: B");
}
else
{
    Console.WriteLine("Grade: C");
}
```

- The program evaluates the score and prints the grade accordingly.

3. switch Statement

The `switch` statement is an alternative to multiple `if-else` statements when you need to compare a single variable to multiple values. It's more efficient and readable when dealing with multiple options.

```csharp
Copy
int dayOfWeek = 3;
```

```
switch (dayOfWeek)
{
    case 1:
        Console.WriteLine("Monday");
        break;
    case 2:
        Console.WriteLine("Tuesday");
        break;
    case 3:
        Console.WriteLine("Wednesday");
        break;
    default:
        Console.WriteLine("Invalid day");
        break;
}
```

- The switch statement evaluates dayOfWeek and matches it with the corresponding case block.

Loops: for, while, foreach

Loops allow you to repeat a block of code multiple times, which is essential when working with collections or performing repetitive tasks.

1. for Loop

The for loop is the most commonly used loop when the number of iterations is known beforehand. It consists of three parts: initialization, condition, and increment/decrement.

```csharp
Copy
for (int i = 0; i < 5; i++)
{
    Console.WriteLine($"Iteration {i + 1}");
```

```
}
```

- The loop starts with `i = 0`, checks if `i < 5`, executes the code inside the loop, and then increments `i` by 1 in each iteration.

2. while Loop

The `while` loop continues to execute as long as the specified condition remains true. It's useful when you don't know how many times the loop will run ahead of time.

```csharp
Copy
int i = 0;
while (i < 5)
{
    Console.WriteLine($"Iteration {i + 1}");
    i++;
}
```

- The loop continues to run until `i` reaches 5, checking the condition before every iteration.

3. foreach Loop

The `foreach` loop is specifically designed to iterate over collections like arrays, lists, or dictionaries. It's more readable and less error-prone compared to other loops when working with collections.

```csharp
Copy
string[] fruits = { "Apple", "Banana", "Cherry" };

foreach (string fruit in fruits)
{
```

```
    Console.WriteLine(fruit);
}
```

- The loop automatically iterates over each element in the fruits array, making it ideal for collection traversal.

Exception Handling: try, catch, and Custom Exceptions

Exception handling is a mechanism in C# to handle runtime errors and ensure that your program doesn't crash when unexpected situations arise. It allows you to catch errors and take corrective actions.

1. try and catch

The try block contains the code that might throw an exception, and the catch block defines what to do when an exception occurs.

```csharp
Copy
try
{
    int result = 10 / 0;
}
catch (DivideByZeroException ex)
{
    Console.WriteLine("Error: Division by zero
is not allowed.");
}
```

- If a division by zero occurs inside the try block, the catch block will handle the exception and print a message instead of crashing the program.

2. Multiple catch Blocks

You can have multiple `catch` blocks to handle different types of exceptions.

```csharp
Copy
try
{
    string input = null;
    int length = input.Length;   // Will throw a
NullReferenceException
}
catch (NullReferenceException ex)
{
    Console.WriteLine("Error:  Object  reference
not set to an instance of an object.");
}
catch (Exception ex)
{
    Console.WriteLine("An     unexpected     error
occurred.");
}
```

- The program first checks for a `NullReferenceException` and then catches any other general exceptions.

3. finally Block

The `finally` block is used to define code that will always run, regardless of whether an exception was thrown or not. It's commonly used for clean-up actions (e.g., closing files or releasing resources).

```csharp
Copy
try
{
```

44

```
    Console.WriteLine("Processing data...");
}
catch (Exception ex)
{
    Console.WriteLine($"Error: {ex.Message}");
}
finally
{
    Console.WriteLine("Cleanup code executed.");
}
```

- The `finally` block ensures that the cleanup code runs whether or not an exception occurs.

4. Custom Exceptions

You can define your own exceptions by creating a class that inherits from `Exception`. This is useful when you need to handle specific errors in your application.

```csharp
Copy
public class InvalidAgeException : Exception
{
    public InvalidAgeException(string message) :
base(message) { }
}

public class Person
{
    public int Age { get; set; }

    public void SetAge(int age)
    {
        if (age < 0)
        {
            throw new InvalidAgeException("Age
cannot be negative.");
        }
        Age = age;
    }
```

}

- In this example, we've defined a custom exception `InvalidAgeException` to handle invalid age inputs.

Real-World Example: Handling User Input Errors in a Form Submission System

Let's create a simple form submission system where the user enters their name and age. We will handle user input errors like invalid age or empty fields using control flow and exception handling.

Step 1: Define the User Input Form

We'll start by creating a `UserForm` class that simulates receiving input from the user.

```csharp
Copy
public class UserForm
{
    public string Name { get; set; }
    public int Age { get; set; }

    public void SubmitForm(string name, string ageInput)
    {
        if (string.IsNullOrWhiteSpace(name))
        {
            throw new ArgumentException("Name cannot be empty.");
        }

        if (!int.TryParse(ageInput, out int age) || age <= 0)
        {
```

```
         throw   new   InvalidAgeException("Age
must be a positive number.");
      }

      Name = name;
      Age = age;

      Console.WriteLine($"Form          submitted
successfully: {Name}, Age: {Age}");
   }
}
```

- The method SubmitForm checks if the name is empty and if the age is a valid positive number.

Step 2: Handle Errors in the Main Program

Now, we'll handle exceptions in the Main method using try-catch blocks.

```csharp
Copy
class Program
{
    static void Main()
    {
        var userForm = new UserForm();

        Console.WriteLine("Enter your name:");
        string name = Console.ReadLine();

        Console.WriteLine("Enter your age:");
        string age = Console.ReadLine();

        try
        {
            userForm.SubmitForm(name, age);
        }
        catch (ArgumentException ex)
        {
```

```
        Console.WriteLine($"Error:
{ex.Message}");
        }
        catch (InvalidAgeException ex)
        {
            Console.WriteLine($"Error:
{ex.Message}");
        }
        catch (Exception ex)
        {
            Console.WriteLine($"Unexpected
error: {ex.Message}");
        }
    }
}
```

Output:

```yaml
yaml
Copy
Enter your name:
John
Enter your age:
-5
Error: Age must be a positive number.
```

- In this example, if the user enters an invalid name or age, the exception handling system ensures that the program doesn't crash and instead provides a helpful error message.

Best Practices for Control Flow and Exception Handling

1. **Use Exception Handling Sparingly**: Exceptions should be used for exceptional situations, not for normal control flow. Use control flow statements like `if` and `switch` for expected conditions.

2. **Be Specific with Catch Blocks**: Catch specific exceptions first, followed by general ones. This allows you to handle different types of errors in the most appropriate way.
3. **Validate Inputs Early**: Before performing operations like parsing or processing user input, validate the data to prevent exceptions from occurring in the first place.
4. **Avoid Empty Catch Blocks**: Always handle or log exceptions. An empty `catch` block may hide bugs or leave your application in an inconsistent state.
5. **Always Clean Up Resources**: Use the `finally` block or `using` statements to ensure resources like file handles, database connections, or network streams are properly closed or disposed of.

This chapter covers the essential concepts of control flow and exception handling, with real-world examples that show how to manage user input errors in a form submission system. It demonstrates how to use conditional statements, loops, and exception handling effectively to create robust and user-friendly applications.

CHAPTER FIVE

Working with LINQ (Language Integrated Query)

Introduction to LINQ: What It Is and Why It's Useful

Language Integrated Query (LINQ) is a powerful feature in C# that allows developers to query various data sources (such as arrays, collections, databases, and XML) in a consistent way using C# syntax. LINQ integrates query capabilities directly into the C# language, which helps make querying data more intuitive and expressive.

What Makes LINQ Useful?

1. **Concise Syntax**: LINQ enables developers to write SQL-like queries directly in C# code, reducing the need for multiple iterations and manual filtering.
2. **Uniform Querying Across Data Sources**: You can use the same query syntax to work with different types of data, whether it's a collection of objects, XML, or a database.
3. **Readability**: LINQ provides a more readable and declarative way to express queries compared to traditional loops and conditionals.
4. **Strongly Typed**: LINQ queries are checked at compile time, ensuring that they are type-safe and reducing errors during runtime.

LINQ Basics

LINQ queries are typically used with the following LINQ operators:

- **from**: Starts the query and defines the data source.
- **where**: Filters data based on a condition.
- **select**: Projects data into a new form.
- **orderby**: Sorts data in a specified order.
- **group by**: Groups data into sets.

LINQ queries can be written in two primary syntaxes:

- **Query Syntax**: Similar to SQL, using from, where, select, etc.
- **Method Syntax**: Uses method calls like .Where(), .Select(), .OrderBy(), etc.

LINQ Queries: Filtering, Projecting, and Sorting Data

1. Filtering Data with LINQ

The where clause in LINQ allows you to filter data based on conditions. It's similar to the WHERE clause in SQL.

Example: Filter a list of integers to only include even numbers.

```csharp
Copy
List<int> numbers = new List<int> { 1, 2, 3, 4,
5, 6, 7, 8, 9, 10 };

var evenNumbers = from n in numbers
                  where n % 2 == 0
                  select n;
```

```
foreach (var num in evenNumbers)
{
    Console.WriteLine(num);
}
```

- **Output**:

  ```
  Copy
  2
  4
  6
  8
  10
  ```

- In this example, the `where` clause filters the numbers list to include only even numbers.

2. Projecting Data with LINQ

Projection is the process of transforming data into a new form, typically using the `select` keyword. This allows you to retrieve specific properties or fields from the original data.

Example: Project a list of `Person` objects into a list of strings with their names.

```csharp
Copy
public class Person
{
    public string Name { get; set; }
    public int Age { get; set; }
}

List<Person> people = new List<Person>
{
    new Person { Name = "Alice", Age = 30 },
    new Person { Name = "Bob", Age = 25 },
```

```
    new Person { Name = "Charlie", Age = 35 }
};

var names = from p in people
            select p.Name;

foreach (var name in names)
{
    Console.WriteLine(name);
}
```

- **Output**:

```
Copy
Alice
Bob
Charlie
```

- The `select` clause projects the `Name` property of each `Person` object into a new list of strings.

3. Sorting Data with LINQ

The `orderby` clause allows you to sort data by one or more fields. You can also sort in descending order using `descending`.

Example: Sort a list of `Person` objects by age in ascending order.

```csharp
Copy
var sortedPeople = from p in people
                   orderby p.Age
                   select p;

foreach (var person in sortedPeople)
{
```

```
    Console.WriteLine($"{person.Name},        Age:
{person.Age}");
}
```

- **Output**:

  ```
  yaml
  Copy
  Bob, Age: 25
  Alice, Age: 30
  Charlie, Age: 35
  ```

- The orderby clause sorts the people list by the Age property.

Example: Sort by age in descending order.

```csharp
csharp
Copy
var sortedPeopleDesc = from p in people
                       orderby p.Age descending
                       select p;

foreach (var person in sortedPeopleDesc)
{
    Console.WriteLine($"{person.Name},        Age:
{person.Age}");
}
```

- **Output**:

  ```
  yaml
  Copy
  Charlie, Age: 35
  Alice, Age: 30
  Bob, Age: 25
  ```

4. Combining Filters, Projections, and Sorting

You can combine multiple operations (filtering, projecting, and sorting) in a single LINQ query.

Example: Find all people over 30 years old, sort by name, and project their names.

```csharp
Copy
var result = from p in people
             where p.Age > 30
             orderby p.Name
             select p.Name;

foreach (var name in result)
{
    Console.WriteLine(name);
}
```

- **Output**:

    ```
    Copy
    Charlie
    ```

Real-World Example: Querying Data from a Database or File System

In this section, we'll see how LINQ can be applied to real-world data, such as querying data from a database or a file system. We'll demonstrate how LINQ can simplify queries that are typically more complex when using traditional methods.

1. Querying Data from a Database with LINQ to SQL

LINQ can be used to query databases, making it easier to retrieve data without writing complex SQL queries. Below is an example that demonstrates how to use **LINQ to SQL**.

```csharp
Copy
using (var context = new MyDatabaseContext())
{
    var query = from customer in context.Customers
                where customer.City == "New York"
                orderby customer.LastName
                select customer;

    foreach (var customer in query)
    {
        Console.WriteLine($"{customer.FirstName} {customer.LastName}");
    }
}
```

- **Explanation**:
  - `context.Customers` represents a collection of customers in the database.
  - The `where` clause filters customers who live in New York.
  - The `orderby` clause sorts them by last name.

2. Querying Data from a File System with LINQ to Objects

LINQ can also be used to query file system data. Let's say we have a list of file paths, and we want to filter out all `.txt` files and sort them alphabetically.

csharp

```
Copy
string[]                     files                   =
Directory.GetFiles(@"C:\SomeDirectory");

var textFiles = from file in files
               where file.EndsWith(".txt")
               orderby file
               select file;

foreach (var file in textFiles)
{
    Console.WriteLine(file);
}
```

- **Explanation**:
  - ∩ `Directory.GetFiles()` retrieves all file paths in the specified directory.
  - o The `where` clause filters the list to include only `.txt` files.
  - o The `orderby` clause sorts the file paths alphabetically.

3. Using LINQ with XML Data

LINQ to XML makes it easy to query XML documents. Below is an example of how to query an XML file using LINQ.

```csharp
Copy
XDocument            xmlDoc            =
XDocument.Load("employees.xml");

var    employees   =    from    emp    in
xmlDoc.Descendants("Employee")
            where (int)emp.Element("Age") >
30
            orderby
(string)emp.Element("LastName")
            select new
```

```
                {
                    Name                          =
(string)emp.Element("FirstName")   +   "   "   +
(string)emp.Element("LastName"),
                    Age                           =
(int)emp.Element("Age")
                };

foreach (var emp in employees)
{
    Console.WriteLine($"{emp.Name},           Age:
{emp.Age}");
}
```

- **Explanation**:
  - o XDocument.Load() loads the XML file.
  - o Descendants("Employee") returns all Employee elements from the XML.
  - o The where clause filters employees over the age of 30.
  - o The orderby clause sorts them by last name.
  - o The result is projected into a new anonymous type containing the full name and age.

Best Practices for Using LINQ

1. **Use LINQ When Queries Are Simple**: LINQ is great for expressing simple data queries. For more complex scenarios, consider using stored procedures or other optimized database access methods.
2. **Avoid Repeated Queries**: When querying large datasets, avoid repeating queries multiple times. Store the results in a variable if you need to reuse them.
3. **Use Method Syntax for Composability**: LINQ's method syntax allows you to chain multiple

operators together, making it easy to compose queries dynamically.

4. **Be Mindful of Performance**: While LINQ provides an expressive syntax, it can sometimes be less efficient than traditional loops or database queries. Always profile performance if you're working with large datasets.

5. **Use Deferred Execution with Care**: LINQ queries typically use deferred execution, meaning they aren't executed until you iterate over them. Be cautious when passing LINQ queries around to avoid unexpected behavior.

This chapter introduced LINQ and demonstrated how it can be used to filter, project, and sort data, as well as its application in real-world scenarios such as querying a database, a file system, and XML data. LINQ simplifies querying operations and makes your code more readable and maintainable.

CHAPTER SIX

Implementing Asynchronous Programming in C#

Why Asynchronous Programming?

Asynchronous programming allows a program to perform tasks concurrently, improving responsiveness and performance, especially in applications that deal with I/O-bound operations like file handling, web requests, and database queries.

Benefits of Asynchronous Programming:

1. **Improved Responsiveness**: In user interfaces (UI) or web servers, asynchronous programming allows the application to remain responsive while long-running tasks are executed in the background. For example, a web application can continue serving requests while it fetches data from a database asynchronously.
2. **Better Resource Utilization**: Asynchronous programming helps maximize CPU and network efficiency by freeing up resources while waiting for I/O operations, rather than blocking the entire thread. This is especially important in high-performance applications like web servers or mobile apps.
3. **Non-blocking Operations**: With asynchronous programming, threads aren't blocked while waiting for operations to complete. This helps to avoid

freezing or lagging in applications that need to handle many tasks concurrently.

Common Use Cases for Asynchronous Programming:

- **File I/O**: Reading or writing files asynchronously to avoid blocking the main thread.
- **Web Requests**: Making HTTP requests without blocking the main thread (e.g., fetching data from an API).
- **Database Queries**: Performing database queries asynchronously so the application can continue processing other tasks.
- **UI Applications**: Keeping a UI responsive while performing lengthy background tasks.

---

async and await Keywords

In C#, asynchronous programming is implemented using the `async` and `await` keywords. These keywords make asynchronous programming easier to write and understand by allowing code to execute asynchronously in a synchronous-like manner.

1. The `async` Keyword

The `async` keyword is applied to a method to indicate that it will perform asynchronous operations. It modifies the method to allow the use of the `await` keyword within the method.

```csharp
Copy
public async Task<int> FetchDataAsync()
{
```

```
    // Simulating an asynchronous operation like
downloading data.
    await Task.Delay(2000);  // Simulates a delay
of 2 seconds.
    return 42;
}
```

- The method must return a `Task`, `Task<T>`, or `ValueTask<T>`. This represents the operation that will eventually complete and yield a result.
- You cannot call `await` in a method that isn't marked as `async`.

2. The `await` Keyword

The `await` keyword is used to pause the execution of an asynchronous method until the awaited task is complete. It tells the program to continue executing other code while waiting for the task to finish.

```csharp
Copy
public async Task<int> ProcessDataAsync()
{
    int data = await FetchDataAsync();  // Waits
for the result of FetchDataAsync()
    Console.WriteLine($"Processed          data:
{data}");
    return data;
}
```

- When `await` is called, it causes the method to return control to the caller until the task is finished.
- `await` can only be used in methods marked as `async`.

3. Running Asynchronous Methods

You can call asynchronous methods using the `await` keyword within other `async` methods.

```csharp
Copy
public async Task RunAsync()
{
    int result = await ProcessDataAsync();
    Console.WriteLine($"Result: {result}");
}
```

- In this example, `RunAsync` calls the `ProcessDataAsync` method and waits for its completion before printing the result.

4. Error Handling with Asynchronous Methods

Asynchronous methods can throw exceptions like synchronous methods. To handle errors, use `try-catch` blocks inside the `async` method.

```csharp
Copy
public async Task<int> ProcessDataAsync()
{
    try
    {
        int result = await FetchDataAsync();
        return result;
    }
    catch (Exception ex)
    {
        Console.WriteLine($"Error:
{ex.Message}");
        return -1;  // Return a default value in
case of error.
    }
```

}

- The error handling is similar to synchronous code, but inside the asynchronous method.

Real-World Example: Building a Web Scraper that Fetches Data Asynchronously

Let's build a simple web scraper that fetches data from a website asynchronously. We will use the `HttpClient` class to fetch data from a website and process the HTML content without blocking the main thread.

Step 1: Install Necessary Packages

Before starting, ensure that the `HttpClient` class is available by including the `System.Net.Http` namespace. You may also need to install the `HtmlAgilityPack` library for parsing HTML, which you can add via NuGet.

```bash
Copy
dotnet add package HtmlAgilityPack
```

Step 2: Define the Web Scraper Class

We'll create a `WebScraper` class that fetches data from a URL and processes it asynchronously.

```csharp
Copy
using System;
using System.Net.Http;
using System.Threading.Tasks;
using HtmlAgilityPack;

public class WebScraper
```

```csharp
{
    private static readonly HttpClient client =
new HttpClient();

    public async Task ScrapeWebsiteAsync(string
url)
    {
        try
        {
            // Fetch the HTML content of the page
asynchronously
            string      htmlContent      =      await
client.GetStringAsync(url);

            // Load  the  HTML  content  into  an
HtmlDocument object
            var       htmlDocument       =       new
HtmlDocument();
            htmlDocument.LoadHtml(htmlContent);

            // Example: Extract all links (anchor
tags) from the webpage
            var             links             =
htmlDocument.DocumentNode.SelectNodes("//a[@href]");

            if (links != null)
            {
                foreach (var link in links)
                {
Console.WriteLine(link.GetAttributeValue("href"
, ""));
                }
            }
            else
            {
                Console.WriteLine("No      links
found on the page.");
            }
        }
        catch (Exception ex)
        {
```

```
        Console.WriteLine($"Error    scraping
the website: {ex.Message}");
        }
    }
}
```

Explanation:

- **HttpClient.GetStringAsync(url)**: This is the asynchronous call that fetches the HTML content from the given URL.
- **HtmlAgilityPack**: This library is used to parse the HTML content and extract relevant information (in this case, the links).
- **Asynchronous Execution**: The method ScrapeWebsiteAsync runs asynchronously, meaning it does not block the main thread while the website is being scraped.

Step 3: Running the Scraper

Now, we'll create a Main method to test the scraper by fetching data from a public website.

```csharp
Copy
class Program
{
    static async Task Main(string[] args)
    {
        WebScraper scraper = new WebScraper();

        Console.WriteLine("Starting          web
scraper...");
        await
scraper.ScrapeWebsiteAsync("https://example.com
");

        Console.WriteLine("Web           scraping
completed.");
```

66

```
    }
}
```

- **Main method**: The `Main` method is marked as `async Task` to allow asynchronous execution. We call `ScrapeWebsiteAsync` and `await` its completion.

Output:

```
arduino
Copy
Starting web scraper...
https://example.com/link1
https://example.com/link2
...
Web scraping completed.
```

Best Practices for Asynchronous Programming

1. **Use `async` and `await` Everywhere**: Always mark methods that perform asynchronous operations with `async`. Use `await` to wait for asynchronous operations to complete without blocking the thread.
2. **Avoid Blocking Code**: Avoid calling `.Result` or `.Wait()` on async tasks, as this blocks the thread and negates the benefits of asynchronous programming.
3. **Handle Exceptions Properly**: Always use `try-catch` blocks inside asynchronous methods to handle potential exceptions, especially when working with I/O operations (e.g., web requests, file operations).
4. **Use `ConfigureAwait(false)` in Library Code**: When writing libraries, use `.ConfigureAwait(false)` to avoid capturing the context in ASP.NET applications, which can improve performance.

5. **Cancellation Tokens**: Use `CancellationToken` for canceling long-running asynchronous operations. This is useful when dealing with tasks that might need to be canceled (e.g., canceling a web request when a user cancels an operation).

This chapter covered the basics of asynchronous programming in C# using the `async` and `await` keywords, explained why asynchronous programming is important, and demonstrated how to use asynchronous methods in a real-world web scraper example. By incorporating asynchronous programming into your applications, you can significantly improve performance and responsiveness.

CHAPTER SEVEN

Using Delegates and Events

What Are Delegates?

In C#, a **delegate** is a type that represents references to methods with a specific parameter list and return type. Essentially, a delegate allows methods to be passed as parameters, providing a way to define callback methods. They are powerful because they enable event-driven programming and the ability to call methods dynamically.

1. Defining a Delegate

A delegate is defined using the `delegate` keyword, followed by the method signature it represents.

```csharp
Copy
public delegate void NotifyUser(string message);
```

- In this example, the `NotifyUser` delegate can point to any method that takes a `string` parameter and returns `void`.

2. Instantiating a Delegate

To use a delegate, you instantiate it and assign it a method that matches the delegate's signature.

```csharp
Copy
```

```
public class NotificationSystem
{
    public void SendEmail(string message)
    {
        Console.WriteLine($"Email          sent:
{message}");
    }

    public void SendSMS(string message)
    {
        Console.WriteLine($"SMS            sent:
{message}");
    }
}

class Program
{
    static void Main()
    {
        NotificationSystem notification = new
NotificationSystem();

        // Instantiate the delegate with a method
        NotifyUser      notify      =      new
NotifyUser(notification.SendEmail);

        // Call the method via delegate
        notify("Welcome to our platform!");

        // You can change the delegate to point
to another method
        notify                 =               new
NotifyUser(notification.SendSMS);
        notify("Your order has been shipped!");
    }
}
```

- **Output**:

```
vbnet
Copy
Email sent: Welcome to our platform!
```

SMS sent: Your order has been shipped!

- Here, the delegate `NotifyUser` is used to invoke different methods (`SendEmail` and `SendSMS`) dynamically.

3. Multicast Delegates

A multicast delegate allows a delegate to call multiple methods. You can combine multiple methods into a single delegate invocation.

```csharp
csharp
Copy
public delegate void NotifyUser(string message);

public class NotificationSystem
{
    public void SendEmail(string message)
    {
        Console.WriteLine($"Email           sent:
{message}");
    }

    public void SendSMS(string message)
    {
        Console.WriteLine($"SMS             sent:
{message}");
    }
}

class Program
{
    static void Main()
    {
        NotificationSystem notification = new
NotificationSystem();

        // Create a multicast delegate
```

```
    NotifyUser       notify      =       new
NotifyUser(notification.SendEmail);
    notify += notification.SendSMS;   // Add
another method to the delegate

    // Call both methods via delegate
    notify("Account            verification
successful!");
    }
}
```

- **Output**:

```
yaml
Copy
Email   sent:   Account   verification
successful!
SMS sent: Account verification successful!
```

- The += operator allows the delegate to hold references to multiple methods. When invoked, all the methods in the delegate's invocation list are called.

Event-Driven Programming

Event-driven programming is a paradigm where the flow of the program is controlled by events such as user actions (button clicks, key presses), system-generated events, or messages from other programs. In C#, events are built on delegates, where a delegate points to a method that handles the event.

1. Defining an Event

An event is defined using the `event` keyword followed by a delegate type. Events can only be triggered (raised) by the class that defines them, but other classes can subscribe to these events.

```csharp
Copy
public class Button
{
    // Define an event using a delegate
    public event Action<string> Clicked;

    // Method to trigger the event
    public void OnClick(string message)
    {
        // Trigger the event
        Clicked?.Invoke(message);
    }
}
```

- The `Button` class has an event called `Clicked` of type `Action<string>`, which represents a delegate that takes a `string` parameter.
- The `OnClick` method is used to trigger the event.

2. Subscribing to an Event

Other classes can **subscribe** to the event by associating a method with the event delegate.

```csharp
Copy
public class UserInterface
{
    public void ButtonClicked(string message)
    {
```

```
        Console.WriteLine($"Button          clicked:
{message}");
    }
}

class Program
{
    static void Main()
    {
        Button button = new Button();
        UserInterface ui = new UserInterface();

        // Subscribe to the event
        button.Clicked += ui.ButtonClicked;

        // Trigger the event
        button.OnClick("Submit        button        was
clicked.");
    }
}
```

- **Output**:

```
less
Copy
Button clicked: Submit button was clicked.
```

- In this example, when the `OnClick` method is called, the `ButtonClicked` method in `UserInterface` is executed because it's subscribed to the `Clicked` event.

3. Unsubscribing from Events

You can unsubscribe from an event when it is no longer needed to avoid memory leaks or unnecessary method calls.

```
csharp
Copy
button.Clicked -= ui.ButtonClicked;
```
74

Real-World Example: Building a Notification System that Responds to User Actions

Let's put the concepts of delegates and events together in a real-world example. We'll build a simple **notification system** that listens for user actions (button clicks) and sends notifications (such as email and SMS) asynchronously.

Step 1: Define the Button Class with Events

We will start by defining a `Button` class with an event that gets triggered when the button is clicked.

```csharp
Copy
public class Button
{
    public event Action<string> Clicked;

    public void OnClick(string message)
    {
        Clicked?.Invoke(message);
    }
}
```

Step 2: Define the Notification System

Next, we'll define a `NotificationSystem` class with methods to send notifications via email and SMS.

```csharp
Copy
public class NotificationSystem
{
    public void SendEmail(string message)
    {
```

```
        Console.WriteLine($"Sending          email:
{message}");
    }

    public void SendSMS(string message)
    {
        Console.WriteLine($"Sending            SMS:
{message}");
    }
}
```

Step 3: Subscribe to the Event

In the main program, we create an instance of `Button` and `NotificationSystem`. We subscribe the `SendEmail` and `SendSMS` methods to the `Clicked` event.

```csharp
Copy
class Program
{
    static void Main(string[] args)
    {
        Button button = new Button();
        NotificationSystem notificationSystem =
new NotificationSystem();

        // Subscribe to the event with methods
        button.Clicked                        +=
notificationSystem.SendEmail;
        button.Clicked                        +=
notificationSystem.SendSMS;

        // Trigger the event
        button.OnClick("User   has   successfully
signed up!");

        // Unsubscribe from the event
        button.Clicked                        -=
notificationSystem.SendSMS;
```

```
        // Trigger the event again (only Email
will be sent this time)
        button.OnClick("User has logged in.");
    }
}
```

Output:

```sql
sql
Copy
Sending email: User has successfully signed up!
Sending SMS: User has successfully signed up!
Sending email: User has logged in.
```

- The OnClick method of the Button triggers the Clicked event.
- Both SendEmail and SendSMS methods are executed initially because both are subscribed to the event.
- After unsubscribing SendSMS, only SendEmail is triggered when the event occurs again.

Best Practices for Using Delegates and Events

1. **Keep Event Handlers Short and Efficient**: Avoid complex or long-running logic in event handlers. If the logic is complex, consider using a background thread or task to handle the work asynchronously.
2. **Use EventHandler Delegate When Possible**: For standard events (like button clicks), use the predefined EventHandler or EventHandler<T> delegates to simplify your code. These delegates are designed for most common event scenarios.
3. **Unsubscribe When Appropriate**: Always unsubscribe from events when they are no longer needed (for example, when a form or window is closed) to avoid memory leaks.

4. **Use Multicast Delegates Carefully**: Multicast delegates are powerful, but they can become inefficient or cause unexpected behavior if too many methods are subscribed. Be cautious about adding too many event handlers.
5. **Check for `null` Before Invoking**: Always check if the event has subscribers (i.e., if it is not `null`) before invoking it. This prevents `NullReferenceException` in cases where no methods are subscribed to the event.

This chapter introduced delegates and events in C#, covering their definition, usage, and role in event-driven programming. The real-world example demonstrated how to use delegates and events to build a notification system that responds to user actions.

CHAPTER EIGHT

Working with Databases in C# (ADO.NET & Entity Framework)

Connecting to a Database: Using ADO.NET and Entity Framework

When building database-driven applications in C#, two common approaches are **ADO.NET** and **Entity Framework (EF)**. Both provide ways to connect to and interact with databases, but they differ in how they handle data access.

1. ADO.NET: Direct Database Access

ADO.NET is a lower-level data access technology that provides a set of classes for working with data from databases. It allows you to manually execute SQL queries and handle the results.

Steps to connect to a database using ADO.NET:

- Establish a connection using `SqlConnection`.
- Create a command using `SqlCommand` to execute SQL queries.
- Use `SqlDataReader` to read the results of the query.

Example: Connecting to a SQL Server Database Using ADO.NET:

```
csharp
Copy
```

```
using System;
using System.Data.SqlClient;

public class AdoNetExample
{
    public void ConnectToDatabase()
    {
        string        connectionString        =
"Server=myServerAddress;Database=myDataBase;Use
r Id=myUsername;Password=myPassword;";

        using (SqlConnection connection = new
SqlConnection(connectionString))
        {
            connection.Open();
            Console.WriteLine("Connected        to
database!");

            string query = "SELECT * FROM
Products";
            SqlCommand        command        =        new
SqlCommand(query, connection);

            SqlDataReader        reader        =
command.ExecuteReader();
            while (reader.Read())
            {
                Console.WriteLine($"Product  ID:
{reader["ProductID"]},                Name:
{reader["ProductName"]}");
            }
        }
    }
}
```

- In this example, SqlConnection opens a connection to
  a SQL Server database, and SqlCommand is used to
  execute a query.
- SqlDataReader reads the results row by row.

2. Entity Framework (EF): Object-Relational Mapping (ORM)

Entity Framework is a higher-level ORM that simplifies database interactions by mapping database tables to C# classes. It allows you to query and update data using LINQ, making database operations more intuitive and object-oriented.

Steps to connect to a database using Entity Framework:

- Install the necessary NuGet packages (`Microsoft.EntityFrameworkCore`).
- Create a `DbContext` class to manage database connections.
- Define `DbSet<T>` properties for each entity (table).
- Use LINQ to query and manipulate data.

Example: Connecting to a Database Using Entity Framework:

```csharp
Copy
using Microsoft.EntityFrameworkCore;
using System;
using System.Linq;

public class ProductContext : DbContext
{
    public DbSet<Product> Products { get; set; }

    protected override void
OnConfiguring(DbContextOptionsBuilder
optionsBuilder)
    {

optionsBuilder.UseSqlServer("Server=myServerAdd
ress;Database=myDataBase;User
Id=myUsername;Password=myPassword;");
    }
```

```
}

public class Product
{
    public int ProductID { get; set; }
    public string ProductName { get; set; }
}

public class EfExample
{
    public void ConnectToDatabase()
    {
        using (var context = new
ProductContext())
        {
            var products =
context.Products.ToList();
            foreach (var product in products)
            {
                Console.WriteLine($"Product  ID:
{product.ProductID},                Name:
{product.ProductName}");
            }
        }
    }
}
```

- The DbContext class (ProductContext) manages the connection to the database, while the DbSet<Product> represents the Products table.
- LINQ is used to query the database, making it easier to work with compared to ADO.NET's raw SQL queries.

CRUD Operations: Creating, Reading, Updating, and Deleting Data

1. ADO.NET CRUD Operations

In ADO.NET, CRUD operations are performed using SQL queries within the SqlCommand object.

- **Create (INSERT)**: Insert data into a table.

```csharp
Copy
string insertQuery = "INSERT INTO Products
(ProductName) VALUES (@ProductName)";
SqlCommand       insertCommand       =       new
SqlCommand(insertQuery, connection);
insertCommand.Parameters.AddWithValue("@P
roductName", "New Product");
insertCommand.ExecuteNonQuery();
```

- **Read (SELECT)**: Retrieve data from the table (already shown in the earlier example).
- **Update (UPDATE)**: Modify existing data.

```csharp
Copy
string updateQuery = "UPDATE Products SET
ProductName = @ProductName WHERE ProductID
= @ProductID";
SqlCommand       updateCommand       =       new
SqlCommand(updateQuery, connection);
updateCommand.Parameters.AddWithValue("@P
roductName", "Updated Product");
updateCommand.Parameters.AddWithValue("@P
roductID", 1);
updateCommand.ExecuteNonQuery();
```

- **Delete (DELETE)**: Remove data from the table.

```csharp
Copy
string deleteQuery = "DELETE FROM Products
WHERE ProductID = @ProductID";
SqlCommand       deleteCommand       =       new
SqlCommand(deleteQuery, connection);
deleteCommand.Parameters.AddWithValue("@P
roductID", 1);
deleteCommand.ExecuteNonQuery();
```

2. Entity Framework CRUD Operations

With Entity Framework, CRUD operations are simplified using LINQ and the `DbSet` methods.

- **Create (INSERT)**: Insert new data.

```csharp
Copy
var newProduct = new Product { ProductName
= "New Product" };
context.Products.Add(newProduct);
context.SaveChanges();
```

- **Read (SELECT)**: Retrieve data using LINQ.

```csharp
Copy
var products = context.Products.ToList();
foreach (var product in products)
{

Console.WriteLine(product.ProductName);
}
```

- **Update (UPDATE)**: Modify existing data.

```csharp
Copy
var            productToUpdate            =
context.Products.First(p => p.ProductID ==
1);
productToUpdate.ProductName    =    "Updated
Product";
context.SaveChanges();
```

- **Delete (DELETE)**: Remove data from the database.

```csharp
```

```
Copy
var          productToDelete          =
context.Products.First(p => p.ProductID ==
1);
context.Products.Remove(productToDelete);
context.SaveChanges();
```

Real-World Example: Building a Simple Inventory Application with Database Support

In this example, we will build a simple **inventory management system** that allows users to add, view, update, and delete products from a database using Entity Framework.

Step 1: Define the Product Entity

First, we define the `Product` class, which represents the product data in the database.

```csharp
Copy
public class Product
{
    public int ProductID { get; set; }
    public string ProductName { get; set; }
    public int Quantity { get; set; }
    public decimal Price { get; set; }
}
```

Step 2: Define the DbContext

Next, we define the `ProductContext` class, which will manage the connection to the database and provide access to the `Products` table.

```csharp
Copy
```

```csharp
public class ProductContext : DbContext
{
    public DbSet<Product> Products { get; set; }

    protected                override                void
OnConfiguring(DbContextOptionsBuilder
optionsBuilder)
    {

optionsBuilder.UseSqlServer("Server=myServerAdd
ress;Database=myDataBase;User
Id=myUsername;Password=myPassword;");
    }
}
```

Step 3: CRUD Operations for Inventory

Now, we implement methods to add, view, update, and delete products in the inventory.

```
csharp
Copy
public class InventoryManager
{
    private readonly ProductContext _context;

    public          InventoryManager(ProductContext
context)
    {
        _context = context;
    }

    // Create (Add a new product)
    public void AddProduct(string productName,
int quantity, decimal price)
    {
        var newProduct = new Product
        {
            ProductName = productName,
            Quantity = quantity,
            Price = price
        };
        _context.Products.Add(newProduct);
```

```csharp
        _context.SaveChanges();
        Console.WriteLine($"Product
{productName} added to the inventory.");
    }

    // Read (View all products)
    public void ViewProducts()
    {
        var              products              =
_context.Products.ToList();
        foreach (var product in products)
        {
            Console.WriteLine($"ID:
{product.ProductID},                Name:
{product.ProductName},              Quantity:
{product.Quantity}, Price: {product.Price:C}");
        }
    }

    // Update (Modify an existing product)
    public void UpdateProduct(int productId,
string newProductName, int newQuantity, decimal
newPrice)
    {
        var          productToUpdate          =
_context.Products.First(p => p.ProductID ==
productId);
        productToUpdate.ProductName          =
newProductName;
        productToUpdate.Quantity = newQuantity;
        productToUpdate.Price = newPrice;
        _context.SaveChanges();
        Console.WriteLine($"Product  {productId}
updated.");
    }

    // Delete (Remove a product)
    public void DeleteProduct(int productId)
    {
        var          productToDelete          =
_context.Products.First(p => p.ProductID ==
productId);
```

```
_context.Products.Remove(productToDelete);
        _context.SaveChanges();
        Console.WriteLine($"Product   {productId}
deleted.");
    }
}
```

Step 4: Testing the Inventory System

Finally, we write the main program to test the inventory system.

```
csharp
Copy
class Program
{
    static void Main(string[] args)
    {
        using     (var     context     =     new
ProductContext())
        {
            InventoryManager   manager   =   new
InventoryManager(context);

            // Add new products
            manager.AddProduct("Laptop",     10,
999.99M);
            manager.AddProduct("Phone",     20,
599.99M);

            // View all products
            Console.WriteLine("\nProducts     in
Inventory:");
            manager.ViewProducts();

            // Update a product
            manager.UpdateProduct(1,     "Gaming
Laptop", 8, 1199.99M);

            // View updated products
            Console.WriteLine("\nUpdated
Products in Inventory:");
```
88

```
        manager.ViewProducts();

        // Delete a product
        manager.DeleteProduct(2);

        // View remaining products
        Console.WriteLine("\nRemaining
Products in Inventory:");
        manager.ViewProducts();
    }
  }
}
```

Output:

```
yaml
Copy
Product Laptop added to the inventory.
Product Phone added to the inventory.

Products in Inventory:
ID: 1, Name: Laptop, Quantity: 10, Price: $999.99
ID: 2, Name: Phone, Quantity: 20, Price: $599.99

Product 1 updated.

Updated Products in Inventory:
ID: 1, Name: Gaming Laptop, Quantity: 8, Price:
$1199.99
ID: 2, Name: Phone, Quantity: 20, Price: $599.99

Product 2 deleted.

Remaining Products in Inventory:
ID: 1, Name: Gaming Laptop, Quantity: 8, Price:
$1199.99
```

Best Practices for Working with Databases

1. **Use Parameterized Queries**: Always use parameterized queries (as shown in ADO.NET examples) to prevent SQL injection attacks.
2. **Use `DbContext` Efficiently**: In Entity Framework, use `DbContext` within a `using` block or as a singleton in dependency injection to manage connections properly.
3. **Avoid N+1 Query Problem**: In Entity Framework, use `Include()` to eagerly load related data instead of querying related entities separately, which can lead to the N+1 problem.
4. **Transaction Management**: For operations that involve multiple steps, use database transactions to ensure consistency and rollback in case of errors.
5. **Migration Management**: Use EF migrations for versioning your database schema, making it easier to track and apply changes to the database structure.

This chapter covered how to connect to a database using ADO.NET and Entity Framework, perform CRUD operations, and provided a real-world example of building a simple inventory application with database support.

CHAPTER NINE

Understanding Dependency Injection and IoC (Inversion of Control)

What Is Dependency Injection?

Dependency Injection (DI) is a design pattern used to implement **Inversion of Control (IoC)**. It allows the injection of dependent objects into a class rather than creating the objects within the class. In simpler terms, DI is about **decoupling** the components in your application to make it more flexible, maintainable, and testable.

Why Use Dependency Injection?

- **Decoupling**: DI helps to reduce the dependency between classes, making them easier to maintain and extend. For example, instead of a class creating its own dependencies, it relies on an external entity to supply them.
- **Testability**: By injecting dependencies, it becomes easier to substitute real implementations with mock or stub implementations, allowing for unit testing.
- **Flexibility**: You can easily swap out implementations without changing the classes that use them.

Basic Concept of Dependency Injection

Imagine a `Car` class that depends on an `Engine` class. Rather than the `Car` class creating its own instance of the `Engine`, we inject an `Engine` into the `Car` class.

```csharp
csharp
Copy
public class Engine
{
    public void Start()
    {
        Console.WriteLine("Engine started!");
    }
}

public class Car
{
    private readonly Engine _engine;

    // Dependency is injected through the constructor
    public Car(Engine engine)
    {
        _engine = engine;
    }

    public void Drive()
    {
        _engine.Start();
        Console.WriteLine("Car is moving!");
    }
}
```

- In this example, the `Car` class depends on the `Engine` class. Instead of creating the `Engine` inside the `Car`, the `Engine` is injected through the constructor.

Types of Dependency Injection

1. **Constructor Injection**: The dependency is passed through the constructor (shown above).
2. **Setter Injection**: The dependency is set via a property or setter method.
3. **Interface Injection**: The dependent class exposes an injection method through an interface.

An **IoC (Inversion of Control)** container is a framework that manages the lifecycle and dependencies of objects. It automatically resolves and injects dependencies when needed, greatly simplifying the management of objects in an application.

What Is IoC?

- **Inversion of Control (IoC)** refers to the reversal of the flow of control in a system. Normally, an object controls its dependencies, but in IoC, the control is inverted, and dependencies are provided externally.
- **IoC Containers** are frameworks that manage object creation and dependency injection. Examples include **Microsoft.Extensions.DependencyInjection** (used in .NET Core), **Autofac**, and **Ninject**.

How Does an IoC Container Work?

- You register your services and their interfaces with the container.
- When you need an instance of a class, you ask the container to resolve the dependencies.
- The container creates the required objects and injects them into the consuming classes.

Example: Using Microsoft.Extensions.DependencyInjection

Let's look at an example of how to use an IoC container to manage dependencies in a C# application.

1. **Install the Dependency Injection package:**

If you're using .NET Core or .NET Framework, you can use the built-in Microsoft.Extensions.DependencyInjection package.

```bash
Copy
dotnet add package
Microsoft.Extensions.DependencyInjection
```

2. **Register Services with the IoC Container:**

In the `Startup` class (or in the main program for simple apps), we configure the IoC container to resolve dependencies.

```csharp
Copy
using
Microsoft.Extensions.DependencyInjection;

public class Program
{
    public static void Main()
    {
        // Set up the IoC container
        var serviceProvider = new
ServiceCollection()
            .AddSingleton<IEngine,
Engine>()
            .AddSingleton<ICar, Car>()
            .BuildServiceProvider();

        // Resolve and use the Car service
        var car =
serviceProvider.GetService<ICar>();
        car.Drive();
    }
}
```

3. Define Interfaces and Implementations:

```csharp
public interface IEngine
{
    void Start();
}

public class Engine : IEngine
{
    public void Start()
    {
        Console.WriteLine("Engine
started!");
    }
}

public interface ICar
{
    void Drive();
}

public class Car : ICar
{
    private readonly IEngine _engine;

    public Car(IEngine engine)
    {
        _engine = engine;
    }

    public void Drive()
    {
        _engine.Start();
        Console.WriteLine("Car          is
moving!");
    }
}
```

- In this example, the IoC container (ServiceCollection) is used to register the Engine and `Car` classes, along with their interfaces. When you call `GetService<ICar>()`, the container resolves the `Car` object and injects the `Engine` dependency into it.

Real-World Example: Implementing Dependency Injection in a Payment Processing System

Let's implement a real-world example where we use **Dependency Injection** and **IoC** to manage a payment processing system. In this scenario, we will have a `PaymentService` that processes payments through different gateways like **CreditCardPayment** and **PayPalPayment**.

Step 1: Define Payment Gateway Interfaces
csharp
Copy
```csharp
public interface IPaymentGateway
{
    void ProcessPayment(decimal amount);
}
```
Step 2: Implement Concrete Payment Gateways
csharp
Copy
```csharp
public class CreditCardPayment : IPaymentGateway
{
    public void ProcessPayment(decimal amount)
    {
        Console.WriteLine($"Processing     credit card payment of {amount:C}");
    }
}

public class PayPalPayment : IPaymentGateway
{
    public void ProcessPayment(decimal amount)
    {
        Console.WriteLine($"Processing     PayPal payment of {amount:C}");
```

```
    }
}
```

Step 3: Define the PaymentService Class
```
csharp
Copy
public class PaymentService
{
    private      readonly      IPaymentGateway
_paymentGateway;

    // Dependency injected via constructor
    public          PaymentService(IPaymentGateway
paymentGateway)
    {
        _paymentGateway = paymentGateway;
    }

    public void MakePayment(decimal amount)
    {
        Console.WriteLine("Payment started...");
        _paymentGateway.ProcessPayment(amount);
        Console.WriteLine("Payment completed!");
    }
}
```
Step 4: Set Up Dependency Injection with IoC Container

In the `Main` method, we will use the IoC container to inject the appropriate payment gateway implementation into the `PaymentService`.

```
csharp
Copy
using Microsoft.Extensions.DependencyInjection;

class Program
{
    static void Main()
    {
        // Set up the IoC container
        var      serviceProvider      =      new
ServiceCollection()
```

```
            .AddSingleton<IPaymentGateway,
CreditCardPayment>()              //        Injecting
CreditCardPayment
            .AddSingleton<PaymentService>()
            .BuildServiceProvider();

        // Resolve and use the PaymentService
        var           paymentService          =
serviceProvider.GetService<PaymentService>();
        paymentService.MakePayment(100.00m);

        // Switch to PayPal payment
        serviceProvider           =           new
ServiceCollection()
            .AddSingleton<IPaymentGateway,
PayPalPayment>()   // Switch to PayPalPayment
            .AddSingleton<PaymentService>()
            .BuildServiceProvider();

        // Resolve and use the PaymentService
again with PayPal payment
        paymentService                        =
serviceProvider.GetService<PaymentService>();
        paymentService.MakePayment(200.00m);
    }
}
```

Output:

```bash
bash
Copy
Payment started...
Processing credit card payment of $100.00
Payment completed!

Payment started...
Processing PayPal payment of $200.00
Payment completed!
```

Explanation:

- The `PaymentService` depends on the `IPaymentGateway` interface. Through dependency injection, we can inject different payment gateway implementations (e.g., `CreditCardPayment`, `PayPalPayment`) into the `PaymentService`.
- The IoC container resolves the dependencies when the `PaymentService` is requested and injects the correct implementation of the payment gateway.

Best Practices for Dependency Injection and IoC

1. **Use Constructor Injection**: Constructor injection is the most common and preferred method for injecting dependencies because it ensures that the class cannot be used without its required dependencies.
2. **Keep Dependencies Minimal**: Inject only the necessary dependencies into a class to maintain loose coupling and ensure that the class remains focused on a single responsibility.
3. **Leverage IoC Containers**: Use IoC containers to manage object creation and resolve dependencies automatically. This reduces boilerplate code and promotes better scalability.
4. **Avoid Static Dependencies**: Static dependencies make testing difficult and create tight coupling. Prefer dependency injection over static references to classes.
5. **Use Scoped or Transient Services**: In IoC containers, use `Scoped` for services that are tied to a specific request or operation, and `Transient` for lightweight services that don't maintain state.

6. **Ensure Proper Lifetime Management**: Be cautious about service lifetimes (Singleton, Scoped, Transient) to avoid issues like memory leaks, especially with objects that hold onto resources.

This chapter introduced **Dependency Injection** and **Inversion of Control** (IoC), explained how to use IoC containers, and provided a real-world example of implementing dependency injection in a payment processing system.

CHAPTER TEN

Building RESTful APIs with C# and ASP.NET Core

What Is a RESTful API?

A **RESTful API** (Representational State Transfer) is a web service that adheres to the principles of REST, a popular architectural style for designing networked applications. RESTful APIs are stateless and leverage standard HTTP methods like GET, POST, PUT, DELETE, and PATCH to interact with resources.

Key Characteristics of RESTful APIs:

1. **Stateless**: Each request from a client to the server must contain all the information the server needs to fulfill the request. The server doesn't store any client context between requests.
2. **Client-Server Architecture**: The client (such as a web browser or mobile app) and the server (which processes requests and manages data) are separate entities that communicate via HTTP.
3. **Uniform Interface**: RESTful APIs use standard HTTP methods and status codes to interact with resources, providing a predictable and uniform interface.
4. **Resource-Based**: Each endpoint in a RESTful API corresponds to a resource, typically represented in JSON or XML format. Resources are accessed via URLs (Uniform Resource Locators).

5. **Representation**: Resources can have multiple representations, typically JSON, which clients can consume.

Common HTTP Methods in RESTful APIs:

- **GET**: Retrieves data from the server (e.g., fetch a list of customers).
- **POST**: Sends data to the server to create a new resource (e.g., create a new customer).
- **PUT**: Updates an existing resource on the server (e.g., update customer information).
- **DELETE**: Deletes a resource from the server (e.g., remove a customer).
- **PATCH**: Partially updates a resource (e.g., update a single field in a customer record).

RESTful URL Design:

- **GET /customers**: Fetch a list of all customers.
- **GET /customers/{id}**: Fetch details of a specific customer.
- **POST /customers**: Create a new customer.
- **PUT /customers/{id}**: Update an existing customer's details.
- **DELETE /customers/{id}**: Delete a specific customer.

Building APIs with ASP.NET Core

ASP.NET Core is a powerful and flexible framework for building web APIs and web applications. It is cross-platform, allowing you to build APIs that can run on Windows, Linux, and macOS.

Steps to Build a RESTful API with ASP.NET Core:

1. **Create a New ASP.NET Core Web API Project**:
    o Open Visual Studio or use the .NET CLI to create a new Web API project.

```bash
Copy
dotnet new webapi -n CustomerAPI
cd CustomerAPI
```

2. **Define Models (Entities)**: Models represent the data structures that the API works with. For example, we can create a `Customer` model to represent a customer entity.

```csharp
Copy
public class Customer
{
    public int Id { get; set; }
    public string Name { get; set; }
    public string Email { get; set; }
}
```

3. **Create a Controller**: In ASP.NET Core, controllers handle HTTP requests. A controller for a RESTful API usually contains methods mapped to HTTP verbs (GET, POST, PUT, DELETE).

```csharp
Copy
using Microsoft.AspNetCore.Mvc;
using System.Collections.Generic;
using System.Linq;

[Route("api/[controller]")]
[ApiController]
```

```csharp
public class CustomersController :
ControllerBase
{
    private static List<Customer>
customers = new List<Customer>
    {
        new Customer { Id = 1, Name =
"Alice", Email = "alice@example.com" },
        new Customer { Id = 2, Name =
"Bob", Email = "bob@example.com" }
    };

    // GET: api/customers
    [HttpGet]
    public
ActionResult<IEnumerable<Customer>>
GetCustomers()
    {
        return Ok(customers);
    }

    // GET: api/customers/1
    [HttpGet("{id}")]
    public          ActionResult<Customer>
GetCustomer(int id)
    {
        var          customer          =
customers.FirstOrDefault(c => c.Id == id);
        if (customer == null)
            return NotFound();
        return Ok(customer);
    }

    // POST: api/customers
    [HttpPost]
    public          ActionResult<Customer>
CreateCustomer(Customer customer)
    {
        customer.Id = customers.Max(c =>
c.Id) + 1;
        customers.Add(customer);
```

```
        return
CreatedAtAction(nameof(GetCustomer), new {
id = customer.Id }, customer);
    }


    // PUT: api/customers/1
    [HttpPut("{id}")]
    public          ActionResult<Customer>
UpdateCustomer(int id, Customer customer)
    {
        var      existingCustomer      =
customers.FirstOrDefault(c => c.Id == id);
        if (existingCustomer == null)
            return NotFound();

        existingCustomer.Name          =
customer.Name;
        existingCustomer.Email          =
customer.Email;
        return Ok(existingCustomer);
    }

    // DELETE: api/customers/1
    [HttpDelete("{id}")]
    public ActionResult DeleteCustomer(int
id)
    {
        var          customer          =
customers.FirstOrDefault(c => c.Id == id);
        if (customer == null)
            return NotFound();

        customers.Remove(customer);
        return NoContent();
    }
}
```

- o **GET /customers**: Returns a list of all customers.
- o **GET /customers/{id}**: Returns a single customer based on the id.
- o **POST /customers**: Creates a new customer.

- o **PUT /customers/{id}**: Updates an existing customer.
- o **DELETE /customers/{id}**: Deletes a customer by id.

4. **Configure the API in `Startup.cs`**: Ensure the API is properly configured in the `ConfigureServices` and `Configure` methods of `Startup.cs`.

```csharp
Copy
public                              void
ConfigureServices(IServiceCollection
services)
{
    services.AddControllers();
}

public void Configure(IApplicationBuilder
app, IWebHostEnvironment env)
{
    if (env.IsDevelopment())
    {
        app.UseDeveloperExceptionPage();
    }

    app.UseRouting();

    app.UseEndpoints(endpoints =>
    {
        endpoints.MapControllers();
    });
}
```

5. **Run the Application**: Run the API locally using `dotnet run` or by pressing F5 in Visual Studio. The API will be available at `https://localhost:5001` by default.

Real-World Example: Building a Simple Customer API for a Business

Let's build a simple customer management system where users can add, update, view, and delete customers. We will use ASP.NET Core Web API to implement this system with the CRUD operations described above.

Step 1: Create the Customer Model

```csharp
Copy
public class Customer
{
    public int Id { get; set; }
    public string Name { get; set; }
    public string Email { get; set; }
}
```

Step 2: Create the Controller

We already have the `CustomersController` in the earlier example, which provides the basic CRUD functionality.

Step 3: Test the API

Using a tool like **Postman** or **Swagger**, you can test the API's endpoints. Swagger is automatically included in ASP.NET Core projects for API documentation.

- **GET /customers**: Retrieve all customers.
- **GET /customers/{id}**: Retrieve a customer by ID.
- **POST /customers**: Add a new customer.
- **PUT /customers/{id}**: Update a customer's details.
- **DELETE /customers/{id}**: Delete a customer.

Example of a POST Request (to create a new customer):

```bash
```

```
Copy
POST /customers
{
    "Name": "Charlie",
    "Email": "charlie@example.com"
}
```

Response:

```
perl
Copy
HTTP/1.1 201 Created
{
    "Id": 3,
    "Name": "Charlie",
    "Email": "charlie@example.com"
}
```

Best Practices for Building RESTful APIs in ASP.NET Core

1. **Use Proper HTTP Status Codes**: Always return appropriate HTTP status codes for different outcomes:
   - `200 OK` for successful GET requests.
   - `201 Created` for successful POST requests that create a resource.
   - `204 No Content` for successful DELETE requests.
   - `400 Bad Request` for invalid inputs.
   - `404 Not Found` for missing resources.
2. **Use Meaningful Routes**: Design clean and consistent routes for your API endpoints. For example, `GET /customers/{id}` should retrieve a customer by ID, and `POST /customers` should create a new customer.
3. **Versioning Your API**: Consider versioning your API to handle future changes without breaking

existing clients. You can version your API by adding a version number in the route like `/api/v1/customers`.

4. **Document Your API**: Use Swagger or another tool to automatically generate documentation for your API, making it easier for consumers to understand and use your API.

5. **Validation and Error Handling**: Validate input data before processing and provide meaningful error messages. Use custom exception filters or middleware to handle errors consistently.

6. **Security**: Use HTTPS, implement authentication and authorization (e.g., JWT tokens, OAuth), and follow security best practices for API development.

This chapter introduced **RESTful APIs** and how to build them using **ASP.NET Core**. We covered the basics of API development, CRUD operations, and provided a real-world example of building a simple customer API.

CHAPTER ELEVEN

Integrating Authentication and Authorization

Understanding Authentication vs Authorization

Authentication and **Authorization** are two key concepts in securing applications, but they serve different purposes. Let's look at the differences:

1. Authentication

Authentication is the process of verifying the identity of a user or system. It answers the question: **Who are you?**

- **Example**: A user enters their username and password to log in to a website. The server verifies the credentials against a database to confirm the user's identity.
- **Mechanisms**:
  - Username and password
  - Multi-factor authentication (MFA)
  - Biometric authentication (fingerprint, face recognition)

2. Authorization

Authorization is the process of granting or denying access to resources based on the authenticated identity. It answers the question: **What can you do?**

- **Example**: After a user logs in, the application checks their role or permissions (e.g., Admin, User, Guest) to determine which actions they are allowed to perform, such as viewing specific pages or modifying data.
- **Mechanisms**:
  - Role-based access control (RBAC)
  - Claims-based access control

OAuth, JWT, and IdentityServer

OAuth, JWT, and IdentityServer are commonly used technologies for implementing authentication and authorization in modern web applications.

1. OAuth (Open Authorization)

OAuth is an open standard for authorization that allows applications to delegate access to resources without exposing user credentials. Instead of giving a third-party application your username and password, OAuth lets you authorize the third party to access your resources on your behalf.

- **How it works**: OAuth uses an authorization flow where the user is redirected to an authorization server to grant permission. The authorization server then returns an **access token** to the client application, which can use it to make authenticated requests.
- **OAuth Flow**:
  1. The user logs in and grants permission to the client application.
  2. The authorization server returns an access token.
  3. The client application uses this token to access the user's resources from the resource server.

2. JWT (JSON Web Token)

JWT is a compact, URL-safe token format used to securely transmit information between parties as a JSON object. It's commonly used in OAuth as an access token, but can also be used for other purposes, like encoding user claims.

- **Structure of a JWT**:
  - **Header**: Contains metadata about the token, such as the signing algorithm.
  - **Payload**: Contains the claims or user data (e.g., user ID, role, and expiration).
  - **Signature**: Used to verify that the token hasn't been tampered with.
- **Example JWT**:

```
Copy
eyJhbGciOiJIUzI1NiIsInR5cCI6IkpXVCJ9.eyJz
dWIiOiIxMjM0NTY3ODkwIiwibmFtZSI6IkpvaG4gR
G9lIiwiaWF0IjoxNTE2MjM5MDIyfQ.SflKxwRJSMe
KKF2QT4fwpMeJf36POk6yJV_adQssw5c
```

- **Use cases for JWT**:
  - Stateless authentication: JWT can be used for user authentication without needing to store session data on the server.
  - Secure token exchange: Since the token is signed and optionally encrypted, it's safe to transmit across potentially insecure channels.

3. IdentityServer

IdentityServer is an open-source framework that implements OAuth2 and OpenID Connect protocols, providing authentication and authorization services for applications. It integrates well with ASP.NET Core and allows you to set up centralized authentication, manage user identities, and provide secure API access using OAuth and JWT.

- **Key Features of IdentityServer**:
  - o Centralized authentication for multiple applications.
  - o Supports OAuth2, OpenID Connect, and JWT tokens.
  - o Role-based and claims-based authorization.
  - o Extensible and customizable for specific authentication flows.

Real-World Example: Securing an Enterprise Application with Login Systems

In this section, we will build a simple enterprise application with login functionality using **JWT** and **OAuth** for secure authentication and authorization.

Step 1: Setting Up the ASP.NET Core Application

Create a new ASP.NET Core Web API project:

```bash
Copy
dotnet new webapi -n SecureApi
cd SecureApi
```

Add the necessary NuGet packages for authentication:

```bash
Copy
dotnet                  add                  package
Microsoft.AspNetCore.Authentication.JwtBearer
dotnet add package IdentityServer4
```

Step 2: Configure JWT Authentication in `Startup.cs`

We will configure **JWT authentication** in `Startup.cs` so that the application can authenticate incoming requests using JWT tokens.

```csharp
Copy
public class Startup
{
    public                                    void
ConfigureServices(IServiceCollection services)
    {
        // Add JWT Bearer authentication

services.AddAuthentication(JwtBearerDefaults.Au
thenticationScheme)
            .AddJwtBearer(options =>
            {

options.TokenValidationParameters      =      new
TokenValidationParameters
                {
                    ValidateIssuer = true,
                    ValidateAudience = true,
                    ValidateLifetime = true,

ValidateIssuerSigningKey = true,
                    ValidIssuer            =
"https://your-issuer.com",
                    ValidAudience          =
"https://your-audience.com",
                    IssuerSigningKey = new
SymmetricSecurityKey(Encoding.UTF8.GetBytes("yo
ur-secure-key"))
                };
            });

        services.AddControllers();
    }
```

```csharp
    public   void   Configure(IApplicationBuilder
app, IWebHostEnvironment env)
    {
        if (env.IsDevelopment())
        {
            app.UseDeveloperExceptionPage();
        }

        app.UseRouting();

        // Enable authentication middleware
        app.UseAuthentication();
        app.UseAuthorization();

        app.UseEndpoints(endpoints =>
        {
            endpoints.MapControllers();
        });
    }
}
```

- **Explanation**:
    - We add JWT Bearer authentication to the application.
    - We specify the validation parameters, including the issuer, audience, and signing key.

Step 3: Implementing the Login Endpoint

Now, we will create a simple login endpoint that generates a JWT token upon successful authentication.

```csharp
csharp
Copy
public class AuthController : ControllerBase
{
    private readonly IUserService _userService;
// Service to validate user credentials

    public          AuthController(IUserService
userService)
```

```
    {
        _userService = userService;
    }

    [HttpPost("login")]
    public     IActionResult     Login([FromBody]
LoginModel login)
    {
        var              user                =
_userService.ValidateUser(login.Username,
login.Password);

        if (user == null)
        {
            return        Unauthorized("Invalid
username or password");
        }

        // Generate JWT token
        var token = GenerateJwtToken(user);

        return Ok(new { Token = token });
    }

    private string GenerateJwtToken(User user)
    {
        var claims = new[]
        {
            new            Claim(ClaimTypes.Name,
user.Username),
            new            Claim(ClaimTypes.Role,
user.Role),
        };

        var         key        =         new
SymmetricSecurityKey(Encoding.UTF8.GetBytes("yo
ur-secure-key"));
        var creds = new SigningCredentials(key,
SecurityAlgorithms.HmacSha256);
        var token = new JwtSecurityToken(
            issuer: "https://your-issuer.com",
            audience:           "https://your-
audience.com",
```

```
        claims: claims,
        expires: DateTime.Now.AddDays(1),
        signingCredentials: creds
    );

        return                                new
JwtSecurityTokenHandler().WriteToken(token);
    }
}
```

- **Explanation**:
  - o The `Login` endpoint validates the user's credentials using the `IUserService`.
  - o Upon successful validation, it generates a JWT token containing the user's role and other claims.
  - o The JWT token is returned in the response.

Step 4: Securing API Endpoints

Now that we have JWT authentication set up, we can secure other API endpoints by requiring authentication.

```csharp
Copy
[Authorize(Roles = "Admin")]
[HttpGet("customers")]
public IActionResult GetCustomers()
{
    // Only authenticated users with the "Admin"
role can access this endpoint
    return Ok(new[] { "Customer1", "Customer2",
"Customer3" });
}
```

- **Explanation**:
  - o The `[Authorize]` attribute ensures that only authenticated users with the specified roles (in this case, "Admin") can access the endpoint.

Step 5: Testing the API

1. **Login**: Use Postman to send a `POST` request to `https://localhost:5001/login` with the login credentials:

```json
Copy
{
    "username": "admin",
    "password": "password123"
}
```

If successful, you will receive a JWT token.

2. **Access Secured API**: Use the JWT token to make a `GET` request to `https://localhost:5001/customers`. Add the token to the `Authorization` header as `Bearer <your-jwt-token>`.

Best Practices for Implementing Authentication and Authorization

1. **Use Strong and Secure Keys**: Use strong encryption for signing JWT tokens and ensure that the keys are stored securely (e.g., environment variables, secret management services).
2. **Limit Token Lifespan**: Set expiration times for tokens to minimize security risks if tokens are compromised.
3. **Role-Based Access Control (RBAC)**: Implement roles (Admin, User, etc.) to control access to different parts of your application. This can be done using claims in JWT tokens.

4. **Implement Token Refresh**: To avoid having users log in repeatedly, implement refresh tokens that can be used to obtain a new JWT token after the old one expires.

5. **Secure API Endpoints**: Always protect sensitive endpoints by requiring authentication and authorization. Use HTTPS to secure communication.

6. **Keep Authentication Simple**: Don't overcomplicate authentication—use well-established protocols like OAuth2 and OpenID Connect to streamline the process.

This chapter covered how to integrate authentication and authorization in an ASP.NET Core application using **JWT** and **OAuth**. We built a simple login system that generates a JWT token and secured an API endpoint using role-based access control.

CHAPTER TWELVE

Caching Strategies for Enterprise Applications

Why Caching is Important

Caching is a technique used to store frequently accessed data in a temporary storage location, called a cache, to improve performance and reduce the load on databases or other data sources. By storing data in a cache, systems can retrieve it faster, avoiding expensive operations like querying a database, making an API call, or performing complex computations repeatedly.

Benefits of Caching:

1. **Improved Performance**: By retrieving data from the cache instead of recomputing it or fetching it from a slower data source, response times are significantly reduced.
2. **Reduced Load on Back-End Systems**: Caching reduces the frequency and volume of requests to the underlying data sources (e.g., databases), which can improve the overall system's scalability and reliability.
3. **Cost Efficiency**: Reduces the need for expensive database queries, which can be particularly useful in systems that rely heavily on external APIs or have high read-to-write ratios.
4. **Availability**: Cached data can be served even if the primary data source becomes temporarily unavailable, ensuring the application remains functional.

Common Use Cases for Caching:

- **Database Query Results**: Storing frequently queried data in a cache to avoid repeated database queries.
- **Web Pages**: Caching the content of web pages to speed up rendering for users.
- **Computed Data**: Storing the result of expensive computations (e.g., data aggregation or image resizing).
- **API Responses**: Caching API responses to reduce load on external services or APIs.

Types of Caching: In-Memory and Distributed Caching

There are two common types of caching used in enterprise applications: **In-memory Caching** and **Distributed Caching**.

1. In-Memory Caching

In-memory caching stores data directly in the memory (RAM) of the application, allowing for very fast access times. It is typically used for small to medium-sized datasets that can fit in the server's memory.

- **Advantages**:
  - Extremely fast, since it avoids disk I/O and network communication.
  - Simple to implement and manage.
  - Great for data that doesn't change often and needs to be accessed frequently.
- **Disadvantages**:
  - Limited by the amount of memory available on the server.
  - Data is lost if the server is restarted.

- **Example**: ASP.NET Core provides `MemoryCache`, a simple in-memory cache that is easy to set up and use for caching data.

```csharp
Copy
public class ProductService
{
    private readonly IMemoryCache _memoryCache;

    public          ProductService(IMemoryCache memoryCache)
    {
        _memoryCache = memoryCache;
    }

    public Product GetProductById(int productId)
    {
        // Check if product is cached
        if (!_memoryCache.TryGetValue(productId, out Product product))
        {
            // Fetch product from database (simulated here)
            product =
Database.GetProductById(productId);

            // Cache the product for future requests
            _memoryCache.Set(productId, product,
TimeSpan.FromMinutes(10));
        }

        return product;
    }
}
```

- **Explanation**: The `MemoryCache` is used to store the product data temporarily. If the product exists in the cache, it's returned directly. Otherwise, it's fetched from the database, cached, and then returned.

2. Distributed Caching

Distributed caching is used when you need to cache data across multiple servers or systems. Unlike in-memory caching, which is local to a single server, distributed caching allows data to be shared across multiple machines, making it ideal for horizontally scaled systems and cloud applications.

- **Advantages**:
  - o Data is shared across multiple servers, enabling scalability.
  - o Caching is persistent and survives server restarts.
  - o Suitable for large-scale systems or cloud-based applications with multiple instances.
- **Disadvantages**:
  - o Slightly slower than in-memory caching due to network communication.
  - o Requires additional infrastructure to manage the cache (e.g., Redis, Memcached).
- **Example**: Redis is a widely used distributed cache that can store data across multiple machines. ASP.NET Core provides built-in support for Redis caching.

```csharp
Copy
public class ProductService
{
    private readonly IDistributedCache
_distributedCache;

    public ProductService(IDistributedCache
distributedCache)
    {
        _distributedCache = distributedCache;
    }

    public async Task<Product>
GetProductByIdAsync(int productId)
```

123

```
    {
        // Try to get the cached product data
from Redis
        var    cachedProduct    =    await
_distributedCache.GetStringAsync(productId.ToSt
ring());

        if (cachedProduct != null)
        {
            // Deserialize product if it's found
in cache
            return
JsonSerializer.Deserialize<Product>(cachedProdu
ct);
        }

        // Fetch product from database (simulated
here)
        var          product          =
Database.GetProductById(productId);

        // Cache the product in Redis for future
requests
        await
_distributedCache.SetStringAsync(productId.ToSt
ring(), JsonSerializer.Serialize(product),  new
DistributedCacheEntryOptions
        {
            AbsoluteExpirationRelativeToNow    =
TimeSpan.FromMinutes(10)
        });

        return product;
    }
}
```

- **Explanation**: The `IDistributedCache` is used to interact with Redis. If the product is found in the cache, it is deserialized and returned. Otherwise, the product is fetched from the database, cached in Redis, and then returned.

124

Real-World Example: Implementing Caching to Improve Performance in a Large Data-Driven Application

In this example, we will implement caching to improve the performance of an **enterprise-level e-commerce application**. The application handles product listings and uses both in-memory caching and distributed caching to optimize data retrieval.

Step 1: Define the Models

First, we define a simple `Product` class to represent products in our e-commerce system.

```csharp
Copy
public class Product
{
    public int Id { get; set; }
    public string Name { get; set; }
    public decimal Price { get; set; }
}
```

Step 2: Implement In-Memory Caching for Frequently Accessed Data

For quick access to data that doesn't change often (e.g., product categories or top-selling products), we use **in-memory caching**.

```csharp
Copy
public class ProductService
{
    private readonly IMemoryCache _memoryCache;
```

```
    public            ProductService(IMemoryCache
memoryCache)
    {
        _memoryCache = memoryCache;
    }

    public Product GetProductById(int productId)
    {
        // Try to get the product from the in-
memory cache
        if (!_memoryCache.TryGetValue(productId,
out Product product))
        {
            // Simulate database call to get
product
            product                           =
Database.GetProductById(productId);

            // Cache the product for future
access
            _memoryCache.Set(productId, product,
TimeSpan.FromMinutes(30));
        }

        return product;
    }
}
```

- **Explanation**: Products that are frequently accessed (e.g., based on productId) are cached in memory. The cache expires after 30 minutes.

Step 3: Implement Distributed Caching for Shared Data

For data that needs to be shared across multiple servers or instances (e.g., product inventory data), we use **distributed caching** with Redis.

```csharp
Copy
public class InventoryService
```
126

```
{
    private readonly IDistributedCache
_distributedCache;

    public InventoryService(IDistributedCache
distributedCache)
    {
        _distributedCache = distributedCache;
    }

    public async Task<int>
GetProductInventoryAsync(int productId)
    {
        // Check if the inventory count is cached
in Redis
        var inventory = await
_distributedCache.GetStringAsync($"inventory_{p
roductId}");

        if (inventory != null)
        {
            return int.Parse(inventory);    //
Return cached value
        }

        // Simulate fetching inventory count from
the database
        int inventoryCount =
Database.GetProductInventory(productId);

        // Cache the inventory count in Redis for
10 minutes
        await
_distributedCache.SetStringAsync($"inventory_{p
roductId}", inventoryCount.ToString(), new
DistributedCacheEntryOptions
        {
            AbsoluteExpirationRelativeToNow =
TimeSpan.FromMinutes(10)
        });

        return inventoryCount;
    }
```

}

- **Explanation**: Inventory data is stored in Redis to ensure it can be shared across multiple servers. The cache expires after 10 minutes.

Step 4: Combine Caching Strategies for Optimal Performance

In this enterprise application, we use **both in-memory and distributed caching** to optimize performance. Frequently accessed data like product details are cached locally in memory for quick retrieval, while data that needs to be shared across different application instances (like inventory levels) is cached in Redis.

Step 5: Test the Caching System

After implementing the caching, the performance of the application improves significantly, as subsequent requests for the same product or inventory data are served directly from the cache, rather than querying the database each time.

Best Practices for Caching in Enterprise Applications

1. **Cache Strategically**: Not all data should be cached. Cache only data that is read frequently but updated infrequently.
2. **Use Cache Expiration**: Set appropriate expiration times for cached data to ensure it is not stale. Use absolute expiration (e.g., TTL) or sliding expiration based on usage patterns.
3. **Eviction Policies**: Implement eviction policies (e.g., Least Recently Used (LRU)) to manage cache size and remove data that is no longer needed.

4. **Graceful Fallback**: When the cache is unavailable (e.g., due to Redis failure), ensure your application can gracefully fall back to querying the database without crashing.
5. **Monitor Cache Usage**: Regularly monitor cache hit rates and cache performance to identify potential issues and optimize cache size.
6. **Distributed Cache Management**: If you're using a distributed cache, make sure it is properly managed and synchronized across different application instances.

This chapter covered the importance of **caching** and explored different caching strategies such as **in-memory caching** and **distributed caching** using **Redis**. We also built a real-world example to improve the performance of an e-commerce application.

CHAPTER THIRTEEN

Unit Testing and Test-Driven Development (TDD) in C#

What is Unit Testing?

Unit testing is a software testing technique where individual units of code (usually methods or functions) are tested in isolation to ensure that they behave as expected. Unit tests are typically written by developers to verify the correctness of their code before it is integrated with other parts of the application.

Key Concepts of Unit Testing:

1. **Testable Units**: A unit test focuses on testing the smallest part of the application—typically a single method or function. The goal is to verify that the method performs its intended task and handles various edge cases.
2. **Isolation**: Unit tests should be isolated from external dependencies like databases, file systems, or web services. This ensures that the tests are fast, reliable, and repeatable.
3. **Automated**: Unit tests are automated, meaning they can be run frequently to catch bugs early and ensure that code changes do not introduce regressions.

Benefits of Unit Testing:

- **Catches Bugs Early**: Unit testing helps catch bugs early in the development process, reducing the cost of fixing issues later.
- **Improves Code Quality**: Writing tests encourages developers to write cleaner, modular code that is easier to test and maintain.
- **Regression Prevention**: Unit tests act as a safety net when refactoring or adding new features, ensuring that existing functionality still works as expected.
- **Documentation**: Unit tests can serve as documentation for how specific methods or components should behave.

Using xUnit, NUnit, or MSTest

In C#, several testing frameworks are available to facilitate unit testing. Three of the most popular are **xUnit**, **NUnit**, and **MSTest**. These frameworks provide support for writing and running tests, as well as assertions to verify the results.

1. xUnit

xUnit is a popular and modern unit testing framework for .NET. It is known for its simplicity and flexibility.

- **Installing xUnit**:

```bash
Copy
dotnet add package xunit
dotnet          add          package
xunit.runner.visualstudio
```

- **Basic Example of a Unit Test in xUnit**:

```csharp
csharp
Copy
using Xunit;

public class CalculatorTests
{
    [Fact]
    public                              void
Add_TwoNumbers_ReturnsCorrectSum()
    {
        // Arrange
        var calculator = new Calculator();

        // Act
        var result = calculator.Add(2, 3);

        // Assert
        Assert.Equal(5, result);
    }
}
```

- **Explanation**:
  - **[Fact]**: Indicates a test method in xUnit.
  - **Assert.Equal()**: Verifies that the result matches the expected value.

2. NUnit

NUnit is another popular testing framework for .NET, and it offers a rich set of features for unit testing.

- **Installing NUnit**:

```bash
bash
Copy
dotnet add package NUnit
dotnet add package NUnit3TestAdapter
```

- **Basic Example of a Unit Test in NUnit**:

```csharp
csharp
Copy
using NUnit.Framework;

public class CalculatorTests
{
    [Test]
    public                              void
Add_TwoNumbers_ReturnsCorrectSum()
    {
        // Arrange
        var calculator = new Calculator();

        // Act
        var result = calculator.Add(2, 3);

        // Assert
        Assert.AreEqual(5, result);
    }
}
```

- **Explanation**:
    - o **[Test]**: Marks the method as a test method in NUnit.
    - o **Assert.AreEqual()**: Verifies that the result matches the expected value.

3. MSTest

MSTest is the default testing framework for Visual Studio and is integrated with the .NET ecosystem. It works similarly to xUnit and NUnit but with a few differences in syntax.

- **Installing MSTest**:

```bash
bash
Copy
dotnet add package MSTest.TestFramework
dotnet add package MSTest.TestAdapter
```

- **Basic Example of a Unit Test in MSTest**:

```csharp
Copy
using
Microsoft.VisualStudio.TestTools.UnitTest
ing;

[TestClass]
public class CalculatorTests
{
    [TestMethod]
    public                              void
Add_TwoNumbers_ReturnsCorrectSum()
    {
        // Arrange
        var calculator = new Calculator();

        // Act
        var result = calculator.Add(2, 3);

        // Assert
        Assert.AreEqual(5, result);
    }
}
```

- **Explanation**:
    - **[TestClass]**: Indicates that this class contains test methods.
    - **[TestMethod]**: Marks the method as a test method.
    - **Assert.AreEqual()**: Verifies that the result matches the expected value.

Test-Driven Development (TDD)

Test-Driven Development (TDD) is a software development practice where developers write unit tests before writing the actual code. The process follows these steps:

1. **Write a Failing Test**: Start by writing a test for a new feature or functionality that doesn't exist yet. This test should initially fail because the code to make it pass has not been implemented.
2. **Write the Code**: Write the minimum amount of code necessary to make the test pass.
3. **Refactor**: Once the test passes, clean up the code while ensuring that the tests still pass. This step improves code quality without changing the functionality.
4. **Repeat**: Repeat this process for each new feature or piece of functionality.

TDD Cycle:

1. **Red**: Write a failing test.
2. **Green**: Write just enough code to make the test pass.
3. **Refactor**: Refactor the code to improve quality while keeping the tests green (passing).

Real-World Example: Writing Tests for a Business Logic Layer in an Application

In this example, we'll write tests for a simple **payment processing system** that includes a business logic layer. The system needs to calculate the total price for an order, including tax and discounts.

Step 1: Define the Business Logic (Payment Processing)

Let's start by writing the business logic class that calculates the total price for an order.

```csharp
Copy
public class PaymentProcessor
{
    private const decimal TaxRate = 0.1m; // 10% tax rate

    public decimal CalculateTotalPrice(decimal price, decimal discount)
    {
        var discountedPrice = price - (price * discount);
        var totalPrice = discountedPrice + (discountedPrice * TaxRate);
        return totalPrice;
    }
}
```

- **Explanation**:
  - CalculateTotalPrice: This method calculates the total price of an order after applying a discount and adding tax.

Step 2: Write Unit Tests Using xUnit

Now, let's write tests for the CalculateTotalPrice method using **xUnit**.

```csharp
Copy
using Xunit;

public class PaymentProcessorTests
{
    [Fact]
    public void CalculateTotalPrice_WithPriceAndDiscount_ReturnsCorrectTotal()
    {
        // Arrange
```

```
        var       paymentProcessor      =      new
PaymentProcessor();
        decimal price = 100m;
        decimal discount = 0.2m; // 20% discount

        // Act
        var            result            =
paymentProcessor.CalculateTotalPrice(price,
discount);

        // Assert
        var expected = 88m; // (100 - 20) * 1.1
= 88
        Assert.Equal(expected, result);
    }

    [Fact]
    public                              void
CalculateTotalPrice_WithZeroDiscount_ReturnsCor
rectTotal()
    {
        // Arrange
        var       paymentProcessor      =      new
PaymentProcessor();
        decimal price = 100m;
        decimal discount = 0m; // No discount

        // Act
        var            result            =
paymentProcessor.CalculateTotalPrice(price,
discount);

        // Assert
        var expected = 110m; // 100 * 1.1 = 110
        Assert.Equal(expected, result);
    }
}
```

- **Explanation**:
  - The first test checks if the CalculateTotalPrice method correctly

applies a 20% discount and calculates the total price with tax.

o The second test verifies the behavior when there is no discount, and the total price is calculated with only tax.

Step 3: Run the Tests

Run the tests using your preferred method (e.g., Visual Studio, Visual Studio Code, or the .NET CLI):

```bash
Copy
dotnet test
```

- **Expected Output**:

```mathematica
Copy
Test Run Successful.
Total tests: 2
Passed: 2
```

Step 4: Refactor (if needed)

If you find any issues or areas of improvement during testing, you can refactor the code to improve its structure or performance. After refactoring, rerun the tests to ensure everything still works correctly.

Best Practices for Unit Testing and TDD

1. **Write Small, Focused Tests**: Each test should focus on a small unit of functionality and test it in isolation. Avoid testing too many things in one test.

2. **Test Edge Cases**: Ensure that you test edge cases, such as invalid input or boundary values (e.g., zero or negative numbers).

3. **Use Mocking**: When testing classes that depend on external services (e.g., databases, APIs), use mocking frameworks like **Moq** to simulate dependencies and control test scenarios.

4. **Keep Tests Fast**: Unit tests should run quickly, so avoid time-consuming operations like database access or file I/O in your tests. Use in-memory data or mocks.

5. **Refactor Test Code**: Just as with production code, test code should be kept clean and well-organized. Avoid duplicating test logic and use setup methods where needed.

6. **Run Tests Frequently**: Running tests frequently during development helps catch bugs early. Integrate unit tests into your CI/CD pipeline to ensure continuous validation.

This chapter introduced **unit testing** and **Test-Driven Development (TDD)**, discussed popular testing frameworks like **xUnit**, **NUnit**, and **MSTest**, and provided a real-world example of writing unit tests for business logic.

CHAPTER FOURTEEN

Working with Design Patterns

Introduction to Design Patterns: Singleton, Factory, Observer, and More

Design patterns are reusable solutions to common problems that arise in software design. They provide standard ways to solve recurring problems, improving code quality, scalability, and maintainability. Design patterns capture best practices in object-oriented programming, providing developers with proven methods to structure their code efficiently.

1. Singleton Pattern

The **Singleton** pattern ensures that a class has only one instance throughout the application's lifecycle and provides a global point of access to that instance.

- **Use Case**: Useful when you need to manage shared resources like logging, configuration, or database connections where only one instance should exist.

```csharp
Copy
public class Singleton
{
    private static Singleton _instance;
    private static readonly object _lock = new object();

    private Singleton() { }
```

```
public static Singleton Instance
{
    get
    {
        lock (_lock)
        {
            if (_instance == null)
            {
                _instance = new Singleton();
            }
            return _instance;
        }
    }
}
}
```

- **Explanation**: The Singleton class ensures that only one instance of the class is created. If the instance doesn't exist, it is created; otherwise, the existing instance is returned.

2. Factory Pattern

The **Factory** pattern provides an interface for creating objects but allows subclasses to alter the type of objects that will be created. It centralizes object creation and abstracts away the specific class that needs to be instantiated.

- **Use Case**: Useful when you need to create objects based on a condition or configuration, without coupling the code to the specific classes that are instantiated.

```csharp
Copy
public interface IPaymentProcessor
{
    void ProcessPayment(decimal amount);
}
```

```csharp
public        class        CreditCardPayment        :
IPaymentProcessor
{
    public void ProcessPayment(decimal amount)
    {
        Console.WriteLine($"Processing       Credit
Card payment of {amount:C}");
    }
}

public class PayPalPayment : IPaymentProcessor
{
    public void ProcessPayment(decimal amount)
    {
        Console.WriteLine($"Processing       PayPal
payment of {amount:C}");
    }
}

public class PaymentProcessorFactory
{
    public        static        IPaymentProcessor
CreatePaymentProcessor(string paymentMethod)
    {
        switch (paymentMethod.ToLower())
        {
            case "creditcard":
                return new CreditCardPayment();
            case "paypal":
                return new PayPalPayment();
            default:
                throw                        new
ArgumentException("Invalid payment method");
        }
    }
}
```

- **Explanation**: The PaymentProcessorFactory class abstracts the logic for creating different payment processors. The client code simply calls CreatePaymentProcessor with the desired payment method.

142

3. Observer Pattern

The **Observer** pattern defines a one-to-many dependency between objects. When one object (the subject) changes its state, all dependent objects (observers) are notified and updated automatically.

- **Use Case**: Useful for implementing event handling systems, where changes to one part of the system need to notify other parts (e.g., in GUIs or event-driven systems).

```csharp
Copy
public interface IObserver
{
    void Update(string message);
}

public class EmailObserver : IObserver
{
    public void Update(string message)
    {
        Console.WriteLine($"Email: {message}");
    }
}

public class SmsObserver : IObserver
{
    public void Update(string message)
    {
        Console.WriteLine($"SMS: {message}");
    }
}

public class NotificationService
{
    private List<IObserver> _observers = new
List<IObserver>();

    public void Attach(IObserver observer)
    {
```

```
        _observers.Add(observer);
    }

    public void Detach(IObserver observer)
    {
        _observers.Remove(observer);
    }

    public void Notify(string message)
    {
        foreach (var observer in _observers)
        {
            observer.Update(message);
        }
    }
}
```

- **Explanation**: The `NotificationService` acts as the subject, and it notifies all registered observers (like `EmailObserver` and `SmsObserver`) whenever a message is sent.

Why Design Patterns Matter in Enterprise Apps

Design patterns are critical in enterprise applications for several reasons:

1. Reusability

Design patterns provide solutions to common problems, allowing teams to reuse well-tested solutions instead of reinventing the wheel. This leads to faster development and more consistent code.

2. Maintainability

Patterns encourage modularity and separation of concerns, making the codebase easier to maintain and update. For instance, the Factory pattern decouples object creation from the rest of the system, making it easier to change the way objects are instantiated without affecting the application logic.

3. Scalability

Patterns like Singleton, Factory, and Observer help design systems that can easily scale. For example, the Observer pattern makes it easy to add new observers without modifying the core logic of the subject.

4. Flexibility

Design patterns allow developers to design systems that are flexible and easy to extend. For example, the Factory pattern allows you to add new payment processors without changing the client code that interacts with the factory.

5. Communication

Design patterns provide a common vocabulary for developers, enabling clearer communication about solutions. For example, when a developer says "let's use a Factory pattern here," others understand exactly what they mean and how to implement it.

Real-World Example: Implementing a Factory Pattern in a Payment Gateway

In this section, we will implement the **Factory pattern** in a **payment gateway** system where we need to support multiple payment methods (e.g., Credit Card, PayPal, Bank Transfer).

Step 1: Define the Payment Processor Interface

We start by defining a `IPaymentProcessor` interface that all payment processors will implement.

```csharp
Copy
public interface IPaymentProcessor
{
    void ProcessPayment(decimal amount);
}
```

Step 2: Implement Payment Processors

Next, we implement concrete classes for different payment processors (e.g., `CreditCardPayment`, `PayPalPayment`).

```csharp
Copy
public class CreditCardPayment : IPaymentProcessor
{
    public void ProcessPayment(decimal amount)
    {
        Console.WriteLine($"Processing Credit Card payment of {amount:C}");
    }
}

public class PayPalPayment : IPaymentProcessor
{
```

```csharp
public void ProcessPayment(decimal amount)
    {
        Console.WriteLine($"Processing      PayPal
payment of {amount:C}");
    }
}

public      class      BankTransferPayment      :
IPaymentProcessor
{
    public void ProcessPayment(decimal amount)
    {
        Console.WriteLine($"Processing      Bank
Transfer payment of {amount:C}");
    }
}
```

Step 3: Create the Payment Processor Factory

Now, we implement the **Factory** class, which will be responsible for creating the appropriate payment processor based on the input.

```csharp
csharp
Copy
public class PaymentProcessorFactory
{
    public      static      IPaymentProcessor
CreatePaymentProcessor(string paymentMethod)
    {
        switch (paymentMethod.ToLower())
        {
            case "creditcard":
                return new CreditCardPayment();
            case "paypal":
                return new PayPalPayment();
            case "banktransfer":
                return                         new
BankTransferPayment();
            default:
                throw                          new
ArgumentException("Invalid payment method");
```

```
        }
    }
}
```

- **Explanation**: The `PaymentProcessorFactory` class is responsible for creating the correct payment processor based on the specified `paymentMethod` string. This encapsulates the logic for choosing the appropriate payment processor and decouples it from the rest of the application.

Step 4: Using the Factory in the Application

Finally, in the application logic, we use the factory to create the correct payment processor and process the payment.

```csharp
csharp
Copy
class Program
{
    static void Main()
    {
        Console.WriteLine("Enter payment method
(creditcard, paypal, banktransfer):");
        string        paymentMethod        =
Console.ReadLine();

        // Create the appropriate payment
processor
        IPaymentProcessor    paymentProcessor    =
PaymentProcessorFactory.CreatePaymentProcessor(
paymentMethod);

        // Process the payment

paymentProcessor.ProcessPayment(100.00m);
    }
}
```

148

- **Explanation**: The user enters a payment method (e.g., "creditcard", "paypal"), and the factory creates the appropriate `IPaymentProcessor`. The `ProcessPayment` method is then called to simulate the payment process.

Example Output:

```bash
Copy
Enter payment method (creditcard, paypal, banktransfer):
paypal
Processing PayPal payment of $100.00
```

Best Practices for Using Design Patterns in Enterprise Applications

1. **Use the Right Pattern**: Don't apply a design pattern just for the sake of it. Make sure the pattern fits the problem you're trying to solve.
2. **Avoid Overuse**: Overusing design patterns can make the code more complex than it needs to be. Apply them where they add clear value.
3. **Keep It Simple**: Sometimes, simpler solutions (like direct class instantiation or basic inheritance) may work just as well without the need for complex patterns.
4. **Document the Patterns**: When using design patterns, it's a good practice to document the purpose and structure of the pattern, especially in larger codebases.

This chapter introduced several key **design patterns** such as **Singleton, Factory**, and **Observer**, discussed their importance in enterprise applications, and provided a real-world example of implementing a Factory pattern in a payment gateway system. Would you like to explore other design patterns in more detail,

CHAPTER FIFTEEN

Handling Multi-threading and Concurrency in C#

Why Multithreading?

Multithreading is a programming technique that allows an application to run multiple threads concurrently. A **thread** is the smallest unit of execution in a program, and multithreading allows a program to perform multiple tasks simultaneously, improving efficiency and performance.

Benefits of Multithreading:

1. **Improved Performance**: Multithreading allows the application to make better use of multi-core processors, executing multiple tasks at the same time.
2. **Responsiveness**: In UI applications, multithreading ensures that the user interface remains responsive while performing time-consuming tasks in the background (e.g., loading data, making network requests).
3. **Parallel Processing**: Multithreading is ideal for tasks that can be executed independently and simultaneously, such as processing large datasets or performing computations in parallel.

Common Use Cases for Multithreading:

- **Background Processing**: Offloading tasks like file processing or database queries to separate threads to keep the UI responsive.

- **Parallel Processing**: Performing computations across multiple cores (e.g., image processing, data analysis).
- **Server Applications**: Handling multiple client requests concurrently (e.g., web servers, API endpoints).

Tasks and Threads

In C#, multithreading can be achieved using both **Threads** and **Tasks**. However, the `Task` class, which is built on top of the `Thread` class, is usually recommended because it simplifies handling concurrency and provides more functionality, such as better exception handling and cancellation support.

1. Using Threads

The **Thread** class allows you to manually create and control threads. You can start, pause, and terminate threads explicitly.

```csharp
Copy
using System;
using System.Threading;

public class MultithreadingExample
{
    public void PrintNumbers()
    {
        for (int i = 1; i <= 5; i++)
        {
            Console.WriteLine(i);
            Thread.Sleep(1000);      // Simulate
work
        }
    }
```

```
public void RunThread()
{
    Thread          thread      =        new
Thread(PrintNumbers);
    thread.Start();
}
}
```

- **Explanation**: The `PrintNumbers` method runs in its own thread. The `Thread.Sleep(1000)` simulates a delay (e.g., a time-consuming task), and the method prints numbers from 1 to 5.

2. Using Tasks

The **Task** class in C# provides a higher-level abstraction for managing threads and handling asynchronous operations. It is easier to work with and provides a more powerful model for handling parallelism.

```csharp
csharp
Copy
using System;
using System.Threading.Tasks;

public class TaskExample
{
    public async Task PrintNumbersAsync()
    {
        for (int i = 1; i <= 5; i++)
        {
            Console.WriteLine(i);
            await Task.Delay(1000);  // Simulate
asynchronous work
        }
    }

    public async Task RunTask()
    {
        await PrintNumbersAsync();
```

```
    }
}
```

- **Explanation**: The `PrintNumbersAsync` method is asynchronous and uses `Task.Delay` to simulate work without blocking the main thread. Using `await` ensures the task runs asynchronously and the method is non-blocking.

3. Differences Between Threads and Tasks:

- **Threads**: You create and manage threads manually, and they require explicit handling of synchronization and state.
- **Tasks**: Tasks are easier to manage, handle exceptions better, support cancellation, and are more efficient in managing concurrency.

4. Parallel Programming with Tasks

You can use the `Task.WhenAll` method to run multiple tasks concurrently and wait for all of them to complete.

```csharp
Copy
public async Task RunMultipleTasks()
{
    var task1 = Task.Run(() => PrintNumbersAsync());
    var task2 = Task.Run(() => PrintNumbersAsync());
    await Task.WhenAll(task1, task2); // Wait for both tasks to complete
}
```

- **Explanation**: This example runs two `PrintNumbersAsync` tasks concurrently.

153

`Task.WhenAll` ensures that the program waits for both tasks to finish before continuing.

Real-World Example: Handling Multiple File Uploads Concurrently in a Web Application

In this section, we'll implement a **multi-threaded file upload system** where the web application allows users to upload multiple files concurrently. This is a typical scenario in web applications that handle large numbers of file uploads, and multithreading can significantly improve performance by processing multiple uploads simultaneously.

Step 1: Define the File Upload Logic

Let's create a method that simulates a file upload. The method will process each file by waiting for a few seconds (representing the upload process).

```csharp
Copy
using System;
using System.Threading.Tasks;

public class FileUploadService
{
    public async Task UploadFileAsync(string fileName)
    {
        Console.WriteLine($"Start uploading {fileName}...");
        await Task.Delay(3000); // Simulate file upload with a delay
        Console.WriteLine($"Finished uploading {fileName}.");
    }
```

```
}
```

- **Explanation**: The `UploadFileAsync` method simulates uploading a file by using `Task.Delay`. In a real-world scenario, this would be replaced with code that uploads the file to a server or cloud storage.

Step 2: Implement Concurrent File Uploads

Now, we will implement a method to upload multiple files concurrently using **Tasks**. We will simulate this by creating a list of file names and running multiple upload tasks at the same time.

```csharp
Copy
public class FileUploadController
{
    private readonly FileUploadService _fileUploadService;

    public FileUploadController(FileUploadService fileUploadService)
    {
        _fileUploadService = fileUploadService;
    }

    public async Task UploadMultipleFilesAsync()
    {
        var files = new[] { "file1.txt", "file2.jpg", "file3.pdf", "file4.mp4" };

        var uploadTasks = new List<Task>();

        foreach (var file in files)
        {
            var uploadTask = _fileUploadService.UploadFileAsync(file);
            uploadTasks.Add(uploadTask);
```

```
        }

        await   Task.WhenAll(uploadTasks);      //
Wait for all uploads to complete
        Console.WriteLine("All files have been
uploaded.");
    }
}
```

- **Explanation**: We create an array of file names and iterate through them, creating a task for each file upload. We use `Task.WhenAll` to wait for all the file upload tasks to complete.

Step 3: Run the Application

Finally, we implement the main method that initiates the concurrent file uploads.

```csharp
Copy
public class Program
{
    public static async Task Main(string[] args)
    {
        var    fileUploadService    =    new
FileUploadService();
        var    fileUploadController    =    new
FileUploadController(fileUploadService);

        // Upload multiple files concurrently
        await
fileUploadController.UploadMultipleFilesAsync()
;
    }
}
```

- **Expected Output**:

```sql
```

```
Copy
Start uploading file1.txt...
Start uploading file2.jpg...
Start uploading file3.pdf...
Start uploading file4.mp4...
Finished uploading file1.txt.
Finished uploading file2.jpg.
Finished uploading file3.pdf.
Finished uploading file4.mp4.
All files have been uploaded.
```

- **Explanation**: The application starts the upload of all files concurrently. The output shows that all files are processed in parallel, significantly improving the time taken to upload all files compared to a sequential upload approach.

Best Practices for Multithreading and Concurrency

1. **Use `async` and `await` for Asynchronous Operations**: Use asynchronous programming (via `async`/`await`) to avoid blocking threads, especially for I/O-bound operations like file uploads, database queries, or network requests.
2. **Avoid Blocking Calls**: Avoid using synchronous blocking calls (e.g., `Thread.Sleep`, `Task.Wait`) in asynchronous methods, as they can degrade performance.
3. **Handle Exceptions Properly**: Always handle exceptions within each thread or task to ensure that errors in one part of the system don't crash the entire application.
4. **Use Cancellation Tokens**: In long-running tasks, implement cancellation using `CancellationToken`

to allow for safe task cancellation if the operation is no longer needed (e.g., user cancels the file upload).

5. **Limit Concurrent Tasks**: While parallelism can improve performance, too many concurrent tasks can overwhelm system resources. Use mechanisms like a **Task Pool** or **Semaphore** to limit concurrency when necessary.

6. **Synchronize Shared Resources**: When multiple threads access shared resources (e.g., memory, files), make sure to use synchronization primitives (e.g., `lock`, `Mutex`, `Semaphore`) to avoid race conditions and ensure data consistency.

7. **Profile and Benchmark**: Always profile your application to identify performance bottlenecks before using multithreading. Use tools like **Visual Studio Profiler** or **BenchmarkDotNet** to measure the effectiveness of your concurrency approach.

This chapter introduced **multithreading** and **concurrency** in C#, covering basic threading concepts, tasks, and their real-world applications. We implemented a real-world example to handle multiple file uploads concurrently in a web application, improving performance.

CHAPTER SIXTEEN

Building Scalable Applications with Microservices

What Are Microservices?

Microservices is an architectural style where an application is structured as a collection of small, loosely coupled, and independently deployable services. Each microservice is responsible for a specific business functionality and can be developed, deployed, and scaled independently. This approach contrasts with the traditional monolithic architecture, where all components are tightly integrated into a single, large application.

Key Characteristics of Microservices:

1. **Single Responsibility**: Each microservice is focused on a specific task or business capability. For example, a service could handle user authentication, order processing, or payment handling.
2. **Independent Deployment**: Microservices can be deployed independently, which allows for faster releases, rollbacks, and scaling.
3. **Loosely Coupled**: Microservices communicate with each other through lightweight protocols, typically HTTP/REST or messaging systems like Kafka or RabbitMQ. They are designed to operate independently, reducing dependencies.

4. **Decentralized Data Management**: Each microservice typically manages its own data store (e.g., database), avoiding a single shared database across all services.
5. **Technology Agnostic**: Microservices can be built with different programming languages or frameworks, as long as they can communicate using standard protocols (e.g., HTTP, JSON).

Advantages of Microservices:

- **Scalability**: Microservices can be scaled independently based on demand. For example, you can scale the payment service separately from the user management service.
- **Flexibility**: Teams can choose the best technology stack for each service, allowing for optimization based on each service's needs.
- **Resilience**: If one microservice fails, others can continue to operate, reducing the impact of failures.
- **Faster Development**: Microservices can be developed by different teams in parallel, speeding up development time.

Challenges of Microservices:

- **Complexity**: Managing multiple services can become complex, especially when it comes to inter-service communication, data consistency, and monitoring.
- **Distributed Systems**: With multiple services communicating over the network, issues like latency, partial failures, and network errors need to be handled.
- **Data Management**: Managing data across multiple microservices can be challenging, especially when it comes to consistency and integrity.

Building Microservices with C# and Docker

1. Microservices in C# with ASP.NET Core

ASP.NET Core is an excellent choice for building microservices because of its lightweight, modular nature and robust support for RESTful APIs.

To build a microservice in C#, you can follow these steps:

1. **Create a new ASP.NET Core Web API project**:
   o Use Visual Studio or the .NET CLI to create a new web API project for each microservice. Each project will represent one service in your system.

```bash
Copy
dotnet new webapi -n ProductService
cd ProductService
```

2. **Define the Service Logic**:
   o For example, a `ProductService` could handle product-related operations like creating, updating, and retrieving products.

```csharp
Copy
public class ProductService : ControllerBase
{
    private static List<Product> _products = new List<Product>
    {
        new Product { Id = 1, Name = "Laptop", Price = 999.99m },
        new Product { Id = 2, Name = "Smartphone", Price = 599.99m }
    };

    [HttpGet("products")]
```

```
public IActionResult GetProducts()
{
    return Ok(_products);
}


[HttpPost("products")]
public                       IActionResult
CreateProduct([FromBody] Product product)
{
    _products.Add(product);
    return
CreatedAtAction(nameof(GetProducts), new {
id = product.Id }, product);
}
}


public class Product
{
    public int Id { get; set; }
    public string Name { get; set; }
    public decimal Price { get; set; }
}
```

- o This simple `ProductService` exposes endpoints to retrieve and create products.

3. **Add Docker Support**:
   - o Docker allows you to containerize microservices, making them easy to deploy and manage. To Dockerize the service, create a `Dockerfile` in the root of your project.

```
dockerfile
Copy
# Use the official .NET image as the base
image
FROM    mcr.microsoft.com/dotnet/aspnet:5.0
AS base
WORKDIR /app
EXPOSE 80
```

```
FROM  mcr.microsoft.com/dotnet/sdk:5.0  AS
build
WORKDIR /src
COPY
["ProductService/ProductService.csproj",
"ProductService/"]
RUN             dotnet            restore
"ProductService/ProductService.csproj"
COPY . .
WORKDIR "/src/ProductService"
RUN dotnet build "ProductService.csproj" -
c Release -o /app/build

FROM build AS publish
RUN dotnet publish "ProductService.csproj"
-c Release -o /app/publish

FROM base AS final
WORKDIR /app
COPY --from=publish /app/publish .
ENTRYPOINT                      ["dotnet",
"ProductService.dll"]
```

- o **Explanation**: The `Dockerfile` defines the steps to build and run the `ProductService` as a Docker container. It uses the official .NET SDK and ASP.NET Core images to build the application and package it into a container.

4. **Build and Run the Docker Container**:
   - o After creating the `Dockerfile`, you can build and run the container with the following commands:

```bash
Copy
docker build -t productservice .
docker run -d -p 8080:80 productservice
```

- o The service will be available at `http://localhost:8080/products`.

2. Inter-Service Communication with HTTP and RESTful APIs

Microservices typically communicate with each other using RESTful APIs (HTTP/JSON). To enable communication between microservices, you can use **HTTP clients** in C#.

For example, a `OrderService` could call the `ProductService` to retrieve product information:

```csharp
Copy
public class OrderService : ControllerBase
{
    private readonly HttpClient _httpClient;

    public OrderService(HttpClient httpClient)
    {
        _httpClient = httpClient;
    }

    [HttpGet("orders")]
    public async Task<IActionResult> GetOrderDetails(int orderId)
    {
        var productResponse = await _httpClient.GetAsync($"http://productservice/products/{orderId}");
        if (!productResponse.IsSuccessStatusCode)
        {
            return NotFound();
        }

        var product = await productResponse.Content.ReadAsAsync<Product>();
        return Ok(product);
    }
}
```

- **Explanation**: The `OrderService` makes an HTTP GET request to the `ProductService` to retrieve product information. This shows how microservices interact by making HTTP calls to each other's exposed APIs.

Real-World Example: Breaking Down a Monolithic App into Microservices

In this example, we will refactor a simple monolithic application into microservices.

Monolithic Application Structure:

Suppose you have an application where user management, order management, and product management are tightly coupled in a single codebase:

```plaintext
Copy
- User Management
- Order Management
- Product Management
```

Step 1: Identify Microservices

In the microservices architecture, we break the monolithic application into separate services based on business domains:

1. **UserService**: Manages user authentication, registration, and profiles.
2. **ProductService**: Manages product listings, inventory, and product details.
3. **OrderService**: Handles customer orders, order tracking, and payment processing.

Step 2: Refactor Each Component into a Separate Microservice

For example, move the `ProductService` code into its own microservice and containerize it using Docker (as shown earlier).

Step 3: Set Up API Gateway

To manage communication between microservices, we can introduce an **API Gateway** that acts as a single entry point to the entire system. The API Gateway can route requests to the appropriate microservice.

For example, the `API Gateway` can route requests to the `UserService`, `ProductService`, or `OrderService` based on the URL.

```csharp
Copy
public class ApiGatewayController : ControllerBase
{
    private readonly HttpClient _httpClient;

    public ApiGatewayController(HttpClient httpClient)
    {
        _httpClient = httpClient;
    }

    [HttpGet("api/products")]
    public async Task<IActionResult> GetAllProducts()
    {
        var response = await _httpClient.GetAsync("http://productservice/products");
        var products = await response.Content.ReadAsAsync<List<Product>>();
```

166

```
        return Ok(products);
    }

    [HttpGet("api/orders")]
    public     async     Task<IActionResult>
GetAllOrders()
    {
        var     response     =     await
_httpClient.GetAsync("http://orderservice/order
s");
        var     orders     =     await
response.Content.ReadAsAsync<List<Order>>();
        return Ok(orders);
    }
}
```

- **Explanation**: The `ApiGatewayController` acts as an intermediary between the client and the microservices, routing requests to the appropriate service and aggregating the responses.

Best Practices for Building Microservices

1. **Decouple Services**: Each microservice should focus on a single business capability and should be able to operate independently.
2. **Use RESTful APIs**: Microservices typically communicate over HTTP/RESTful APIs or message queues for asynchronous communication.
3. **Service Discovery**: Use service discovery tools like **Consul** or **Eureka** to help microservices locate each other dynamically.
4. **API Gateway**: Use an API Gateway to handle routing, authentication, and other cross-cutting concerns like rate limiting and logging.
5. **Handle Failures Gracefully**: Implement circuit breakers, retries, and timeouts to handle failures between microservices.

6. **Containerization**: Dockerize microservices to ensure consistent environments across development, testing, and production.
7. **Logging and Monitoring**: Implement centralized logging (e.g., using **ELK Stack** or **Prometheus**) to monitor and troubleshoot microservices.
8. **Security**: Implement secure communication between services using HTTPS and OAuth for authorization.

This chapter introduced **microservices** and demonstrated how to build and deploy them using **C#** and **Docker**. We also walked through a real-world example of breaking down a monolithic application into microservices, discussing best practices and tools.

CHAPTER SEVEN

Working with Cloud Services in C# (Azure & AWS)

Introduction to Cloud Computing

Cloud computing is the delivery of computing services (including storage, processing power, networking, databases, software, etc.) over the internet (the cloud), allowing businesses and developers to access powerful resources without the need to manage physical hardware.

Key Benefits of Cloud Computing:

1. **Scalability**: Cloud services can scale up or down based on demand, allowing businesses to adjust resources as needed without upfront investments in hardware.
2. **Cost Efficiency**: With cloud services, you only pay for what you use, eliminating the need for maintaining expensive infrastructure.
3. **Availability and Reliability**: Cloud providers offer high availability and reliability through their distributed data centers, ensuring that applications remain online and resilient to failures.
4. **Global Reach**: Cloud services are available globally, allowing applications to serve users from different regions with low latency.
5. **Flexibility**: The cloud supports a wide range of computing models, including virtual machines, containers, serverless computing, and managed services.

Key Cloud Providers:

- **Microsoft Azure**: A cloud platform by Microsoft offering a wide range of services such as computing, networking, storage, and databases.
- **Amazon Web Services (AWS)**: Amazon's cloud platform, offering a broad set of services for compute, storage, databases, and machine learning, among others.

Using Azure and AWS with C#

In C#, both **Azure** and **AWS** provide SDKs and APIs to interact with their cloud services. These SDKs allow developers to easily integrate cloud services into their applications, enabling features like scalable databases, cloud storage, virtual machines, and serverless computing.

1. Using Azure with C#

Azure offers a variety of services such as **Azure Functions**, **Azure Blob Storage**, **Azure SQL Database**, and **Azure App Services**, among others.

Setting Up Azure SDK in C#:

1. **Install the Azure SDK**: Install the necessary Azure SDK packages via NuGet to interact with Azure services.

   ```bash
   Copy
   dotnet            add            package
   Microsoft.Azure.Storage.Blob
   ```

2. **Connecting to Azure Blob Storage**: Below is an example of how to upload a file to **Azure Blob Storage** using C#.

```csharp
Copy
using Microsoft.Azure.Storage;
using Microsoft.Azure.Storage.Blob;
using System;
using System.IO;
using System.Threading.Tasks;

public class AzureBlobStorageService
{
    private CloudBlobContainer _container;

    public AzureBlobStorageService(string storageConnectionString, string containerName)
    {
        var storageAccount = CloudStorageAccount.Parse(storageConnectionString);
        var blobClient = storageAccount.CreateCloudBlobClient();
        _container = blobClient.GetContainerReference(containerName);
    }

    public async Task UploadFileAsync(string filePath, string blobName)
    {
        var blob = _container.GetBlockBlobReference(blobName);
        await blob.UploadFromFileAsync(filePath);
        Console.WriteLine("File uploaded to Azure Blob Storage.");
    }
```

```
}
```

- **Explanation**:
  - o The `AzureBlobStorageService` class connects to an Azure Storage account using the connection string and container name.
  - o The `UploadFileAsync` method uploads a file to the specified blob container.

Deploying to Azure App Services:

To deploy a C# web application to **Azure App Services**, you can use Visual Studio or the Azure CLI. Here's a quick overview of how to deploy using the **Azure CLI**:

1. Create an Azure App Service:

```bash
Copy
az webapp up --name mywebapp --resource-
group myResourceGroup
```

2. Configure the deployment from Visual Studio:
   - o Right-click on the project in Visual Studio and choose **Publish**.
   - o Select **Azure** and follow the steps to deploy the application to Azure App Services.

2. Using AWS with C#

AWS also offers a wide range of services such as **Amazon S3**, **Amazon EC2**, **AWS Lambda**, and **Amazon RDS**.

Setting Up AWS SDK in C#:

1. **Install the AWS SDK**: Install the AWS SDK for .NET to interact with AWS services.

```bash
bash
Copy
dotnet add package AWSSDK.S3
```

2. **Connecting to AWS S3**: Here's an example of uploading a file to **AWS S3** using C#:

```csharp
csharp
Copy
using Amazon.S3;
using Amazon.S3.Model;
using System;
using System.Threading.Tasks;

public class AWSS3Service
{
    private readonly IAmazonS3 _s3Client;

    public AWSS3Service(string accessKey,
string secretKey)
    {
        var credentials = new
Amazon.Runtime.BasicAWSCredentials(access
Key, secretKey);
        _s3Client = new
AmazonS3Client(credentials,
Amazon.RegionEndpoint.USEast1);
    }

    public async Task
UploadFileAsync(string bucketName, string
filePath, string keyName)
    {
        var request = new PutObjectRequest
        {
            BucketName = bucketName,
            FilePath = filePath,
            Key = keyName
        };

        await
_s3Client.PutObjectAsync(request);
```

```
        Console.WriteLine("File   uploaded
to AWS S3.");
    }
}
```

- **Explanation**:
  - The `AWSS3Service` class initializes an `AmazonS3Client` with AWS credentials and region.
  - The `UploadFileAsync` method uploads a file to the specified S3 bucket.

Deploying to AWS EC2:

To deploy a C# application to **AWS EC2**, you can use **Amazon EC2** instances to host your application.

1. Create an EC2 instance via the AWS Management Console or the **AWS CLI**:

```bash
Copy
aws ec2 run-instances --image-id ami-xyz123 --count 1 --instance-type t2.micro --key-name MyKeyPair
```

2. Deploy your application manually or use CI/CD tools like **AWS CodePipeline** or **AWS CodeDeploy** to automate the deployment.

Real-World Example: Deploying an Application to the Cloud for Scalability

In this example, we will demonstrate how to deploy a simple **order processing application** to the cloud for scalability.

We will break down the process into using **Azure** and **AWS** to deploy a web application.

Step 1: Create the Application:

Let's assume we have a basic order processing API using **ASP.NET Core**.

```csharp
Copy
[ApiController]
[Route("api/[controller]")]
public class OrderController : ControllerBase
{
    private static List<string> _orders = new
List<string>();

    [HttpPost]
    public IActionResult CreateOrder([FromBody]
string order)
    {
        _orders.Add(order);
        return Ok($"Order {order} created
successfully.");
    }

    [HttpGet]
    public IActionResult GetOrders()
    {
        return Ok(_orders);
    }
}
```

Step 2: Deploy to Azure (App Services):

1. **Create an Azure App Service** using the Azure portal or CLI as shown earlier.
2. **Publish the application** from Visual Studio to Azure:
   o Right-click on the project > **Publish** > Select **Azure App Services** > **Create new App Service**.

     o Follow the prompts to publish and deploy the application.

Step 3: Deploy to AWS (EC2):

1. **Create an EC2 Instance** in AWS using the AWS Management Console or CLI.
2. **SSH into the EC2 instance** and install the necessary .NET runtime:

```bash
Copy
sudo apt-get update
sudo apt-get install -y dotnet-sdk-5.0
```

3. **Deploy the application** by copying the application files to the EC2 instance and running the app using the .NET CLI.

Best Practices for Cloud Deployments

1. **Scalability**: Utilize **auto-scaling** features in cloud services (like Azure App Services and AWS EC2) to automatically adjust resources based on demand.
2. **Load Balancing**: Use **load balancers** to distribute traffic across multiple instances of your application to improve availability and reliability.
3. **High Availability**: Deploy applications in multiple regions or availability zones to ensure high availability and fault tolerance.
4. **Security**: Use secure communication (HTTPS), identity and access management (IAM) roles, and encryption to protect your data and services in the cloud.
5. **Monitoring and Logging**: Implement centralized monitoring (e.g., Azure Monitor, AWS CloudWatch) to track application performance and detect issues.

6. **Cost Management**: Keep an eye on cloud resource usage and costs by utilizing cloud cost management tools (e.g., Azure Cost Management, AWS Cost Explorer).

This chapter introduced **cloud computing** and demonstrated how to use **Azure** and **AWS** with C# to deploy applications for scalability. We covered how to deploy a simple order processing application to both cloud providers and discussed best practices for cloud deployments.

CHAPTER EIGHTEEN

Building Web Applications with ASP.NET Core MVC

Understanding the MVC Pattern

The **MVC (Model-View-Controller)** pattern is a design pattern commonly used for building web applications. It divides an application into three main components, each of which has a distinct role:

1. **Model**: Represents the data and business logic of the application. It is responsible for retrieving, storing, and processing data. The model often maps to a database entity or class.
2. **View**: Represents the user interface (UI). It displays data from the model and provides controls to allow users to interact with the application. Views are typically composed of HTML, CSS, and JavaScript.
3. **Controller**: Handles the user input, processes the business logic (with the help of the model), and returns the appropriate view to the user. Controllers are the intermediaries between the Model and the View.

Advantages of the MVC Pattern:

- **Separation of Concerns**: MVC helps separate different concerns of an application. This makes the application easier to manage, test, and scale.

- **Testability**: The separation makes it easier to write unit tests for each component, especially the controller and model.
- **Maintainability**: MVC allows developers to modify the UI, business logic, and data storage independently without affecting the other components.
- **Reusability**: Components like models and views can be reused across multiple parts of the application.

Creating a Simple Web Application

In this section, we will create a simple web application using **ASP.NET Core MVC**. The application will be a basic task management system where users can create, view, and delete tasks.

Step 1: Set Up the ASP.NET Core MVC Project

1. Open Visual Studio or use the .NET CLI to create a new ASP.NET Core MVC project.

   Using the .NET CLI:

   ```bash
   Copy
   dotnet new mvc -n TaskManagementApp
   cd TaskManagementApp
   ```

2. The MVC project template sets up the basic structure of an MVC application, including folders for models, views, and controllers.

Step 2: Define the Model

In the **Models** folder, define a `Task` model class. This class will represent a task in our task management application.

```csharp
Copy
namespace TaskManagementApp.Models
{
    public class Task
    {
        public int Id { get; set; }
        public string Name { get; set; }
        public bool IsCompleted { get; set; }
    }
}
```

- **Explanation**: The `Task` class contains properties for `Id`, `Name`, and `IsCompleted`. This class will map to the data stored in our application (e.g., in memory or a database).

Step 3: Create the Controller

The controller will handle the user requests. In the **Controllers** folder, create a `TaskController` class that will manage the logic for displaying and manipulating tasks.

```csharp
Copy
using Microsoft.AspNetCore.Mvc;
using TaskManagementApp.Models;
using System.Collections.Generic;
using System.Linq;

namespace TaskManagementApp.Controllers
{
    public class TaskController : Controller
    {
```

```csharp
        // In-memory task list to simulate a
database
        private static List<Task> tasks = new
List<Task>
        {
            new Task { Id = 1, Name = "Learn
ASP.NET Core", IsCompleted = false },
            new Task { Id = 2, Name = "Build a
web application", IsCompleted = false }
        };

        // GET: /Task/
        public IActionResult Index()
        {
            return View(tasks);
        }

        // GET: /Task/Create
        public IActionResult Create()
        {
            return View();
        }

        // POST: /Task/Create
        [HttpPost]
        public IActionResult Create(Task task)
        {
            if (ModelState.IsValid)
            {
                task.Id = tasks.Max(t => t.Id) +
1;   // Simulate auto-increment ID
                tasks.Add(task);
                return
RedirectToAction("Index");
            }
            return View(task);
        }

        // GET: /Task/Delete/5
        public IActionResult Delete(int id)
        {
            var task = tasks.FirstOrDefault(t =>
t.Id == id);
```

```
        if (task != null)
        {
            tasks.Remove(task);
        }
        return RedirectToAction("Index");
    }
  }
}
```

- **Explanation**:
    - The `TaskController` manages tasks using an in-memory list to simulate a database.
    - The `Index` action displays all tasks.
    - The `Create` actions (GET and POST) allow users to create a new task.
    - The `Delete` action removes a task by its `Id`.

Step 4: Create Views

In the **Views** folder, create a `Task` folder and add the following views to display and interact with tasks.

1. **Index View** (`Views/Task/Index.cshtml`): This view displays a list of tasks.

    ```html
    html
    Copy
    @model
    IEnumerable<TaskManagementApp.Models.Task
    >

    <h2>Task List</h2>

    <table class="table">
        <thead>
            <tr>
                <th>ID</th>
                <th>Name</th>
                <th>Completed</th>
                <th>Actions</th>
    ```

```
        </tr>
    </thead>
    <tbody>
        @foreach (var task in Model)
        {
            <tr>
                <td>@task.Id</td>
                <td>@task.Name</td>

<td>@task.IsCompleted</td>
                <td>
                    <a
href="@Url.Action("Delete",  new  {  id  =
task.Id      })"        class="btn        btn-
danger">Delete</a>
                </td>
            </tr>
        }
    </tbody>
</table>

<a href="@Url.Action("Create")" class="btn
btn-primary">Add New Task</a>
```

- o **Explanation**: This view displays the tasks in a table, along with options to delete or add new tasks. It uses Razor syntax to loop through the tasks and render them in the table.

2. **Create View** (Views/Task/Create.cshtml): This view allows the user to create a new task.

```
html
Copy
@model TaskManagementApp.Models.Task

<h2>Create Task</h2>

<form asp-action="Create" method="post">
    <div class="form-group">
        <label            for="Name">Task
Name</label>
```

```
        <input   type="text"   class="form-
control"        id="Name"        name="Name"
value="@Model.Name" required />
    </div>
    <div class="form-group">
        <label
for="IsCompleted">Completed</label>
        <input              type="checkbox"
class="form-check-input"  id="IsCompleted"
name="IsCompleted" value="true" />
    </div>
    <button type="submit" class="btn btn-
primary">Create</button>
</form>

<a  href="@Url.Action("Index")"  class="btn
btn-secondary">Back to Task List</a>
```

- o **Explanation**: The `Create` view contains a form for entering the task name and its completion status. When the form is submitted, it posts back to the `Create` action in the controller.

Step 5: Run the Application

To run the application, use Visual Studio or the .NET CLI:

```bash
Copy
dotnet run
```

Once the application is running, navigate to `http://localhost:5000/Task/Index` to view the list of tasks, add new tasks, and delete existing ones.

Real-World Example: Building a Task Management Application

Let's consider a **task management application** that allows users to:

1. **Create tasks** with a name and a completion status.
2. **View all tasks** in a list.
3. **Delete tasks** that are no longer needed.

This task management app is built using the **ASP.NET Core MVC** framework, demonstrating how the MVC pattern is applied in a web application. It includes models to represent the task data, a controller to handle business logic, and views to present the data to the user.

Step 1: Refactor for Real-World Scenarios

For a real-world application, you would typically:

- **Store tasks in a database** (e.g., SQL Server or SQLite) instead of using an in-memory list.
- **Add validation** for task data (e.g., task name length, uniqueness).
- **Implement user authentication and authorization** to secure the application.
- **Use JavaScript or AJAX** to enhance user interaction without full page reloads (e.g., asynchronously adding or deleting tasks).

Best Practices for Building Web Applications with ASP.NET Core MVC

1. **Follow the MVC Pattern**: Use the separation of concerns to maintain clean, modular, and testable

code. Keep your models, views, and controllers focused on their responsibilities.

2. **Use Strongly Typed Views**: Pass strongly typed models from controllers to views to enable better validation and IntelliSense support in the editor.

3. **Implement Validation**: Use **data annotations** to validate input data on the model level, and show appropriate error messages in the view.

4. **Secure Your Application**: Use built-in ASP.NET Core features such as authentication, authorization, and data protection to ensure the security of your application.

5. **Test Your Application**: Write unit tests for your controllers and services to ensure the business logic works correctly, and integration tests to verify your app's behavior end-to-end.

6. **Optimize Performance**: Minimize unnecessary database calls and consider caching frequently used data to improve performance.

This chapter introduced **ASP.NET Core MVC**, explained how to build a simple web application using the MVC pattern, and walked through the creation of a **task management application**.

CHAPTER NINETEEN

Implementing Real-Time Communication in C# (SignalR)

What is SignalR?

SignalR is a real-time communication framework for ASP.NET, providing a simple way to add real-time web functionality to applications. It allows bi-directional communication between the server and client, making it possible for the server to push content to connected clients instantly without the need for the client to constantly request updates.

Key Features of SignalR:

1. **Real-Time Communication**: SignalR enables immediate communication between the server and all connected clients. This is particularly useful for applications that need to display live updates, notifications, or data streams in real-time.
2. **Persistent Connections**: SignalR uses persistent connections, so clients remain connected to the server for as long as they need to receive real-time messages.
3. **Automatic Reconnection**: If the connection is lost (e.g., due to network issues), SignalR automatically tries to reconnect.
4. **Scaling**: SignalR can scale across multiple servers and handle thousands of concurrent connections, making it suitable for high-traffic applications.

Common Use Cases for SignalR:

- **Real-Time Chat Applications**: Instant messaging systems where users can send and receive messages in real-time.
- **Live Notifications**: Push notifications, such as for social media apps, news apps, or sports scores.
- **Collaborative Applications**: Applications like Google Docs where multiple users can collaborate and see each other's changes in real-time.
- **Real-Time Dashboards**: Displaying live data for financial markets, server monitoring, or system health in real-time.

Real-Time Web Applications with SignalR

To use SignalR in a web application, you need to set up both the **SignalR Server** (the backend) and the **SignalR Client** (the frontend). Here's how it works:

1. **SignalR Hub**: A hub is a class in SignalR that acts as the main communication channel between the server and the clients. It allows clients to send messages to the server and the server to broadcast messages to all connected clients.
2. **Persistent Connection**: When a client connects to a SignalR hub, a persistent connection is established, and the client can start receiving real-time updates.
3. **SignalR Client**: On the client side, JavaScript (or any other client framework) interacts with SignalR using a SignalR client library. The client can call methods on the hub and listen for messages sent from the server.

Steps to Set Up SignalR in an ASP.NET Core Application:

1. **Install the SignalR NuGet Package**: Install the SignalR package to use in your ASP.NET Core project:

```bash
Copy
dotnet              add              package
Microsoft.AspNetCore.SignalR
```

2. **Set Up the SignalR Hub in the Server**: Create a SignalR Hub class that defines methods the client can call and methods the server can invoke to send messages to clients.

```csharp
Copy
using Microsoft.AspNetCore.SignalR;

public class ChatHub : Hub
{
    // Method for clients to send messages
to other clients
    public async Task SendMessage(string
user, string message)
    {
        await
Clients.All.SendAsync("ReceiveMessage",
user, message);
    }
}
```

   o **Explanation**: The SendMessage method allows clients to send a message to the server, which then broadcasts the message to all connected clients.

3. **Configure SignalR in Startup.cs**: In the ConfigureServices method, add SignalR services

to the DI container. Then, in the `Configure` method, set up the SignalR route.

```csharp
Copy
public                                    void
ConfigureServices(IServiceCollection
services)
{
    services.AddSignalR();
}

public void Configure(IApplicationBuilder
app, IWebHostEnvironment env)
{
    app.UseRouting();
    app.UseEndpoints(endpoints =>
    {

endpoints.MapHub<ChatHub>("/chathub");
    });
}
```

- ○ **Explanation**: The `MapHub<ChatHub>` method maps the `ChatHub` to the `/chathub` endpoint. Clients will connect to this URL to communicate with the hub.
4. **Set Up the SignalR Client**: In the client-side application, you'll use the SignalR JavaScript client library to connect to the SignalR Hub and send/receive messages.

```html
Copy
<script
src="https://cdn.jsdelivr.net/npm/@micros
oft/signalr@5.0.7/dist/browser/signalr.js
"></script>
<script>
```

```javascript
const          connection     =     new
signalR.HubConnectionBuilder()
      .withUrl("/chathub")
      .build();

// Start the connection
connection.start().catch(err      =>
console.error(err));

// Listen for messages from the server
connection.on("ReceiveMessage", (user,
message) => {
      const msg = `${user}: ${message}`;
      const          li          =
document.createElement("li");
      li.textContent = msg;

document.getElementById("messagesList").a
ppendChild(li);
   });

// Send a message to the server
function sendMessage() {
      const          user          =
document.getElementById("user").value;
      const          message          =
document.getElementById("message").value;
      connection.invoke("SendMessage",
user,          message).catch(err          =>
console.error(err));
   }
</script>
```

- o **Explanation**:
  - connection.start(): Establishes the connection to the SignalR Hub.
  - connection.on("ReceiveMessage", ...): Listens for the ReceiveMessage event, which is triggered when the server broadcasts a message.

- connection.invoke("SendMessag
  e", ...): Sends a message to the server
  to be broadcasted.

Real-World Example: Chat Application with Real-Time Updates

Let's build a simple **chat application** using SignalR that allows users to send messages in real-time to each other. This application will have the following features:

- Multiple users can join the chat.
- Messages are broadcast to all connected users in real-time.
- New users can send messages to the chat in real-time.

Step 1: Set Up the Project

1. **Create an ASP.NET Core MVC Project**: Create a new ASP.NET Core MVC project using Visual Studio or the .NET CLI:

```bash
Copy
dotnet new mvc -n RealTimeChatApp
cd RealTimeChatApp
```

2. **Add SignalR NuGet Package**: Install the SignalR package for ASP.NET Core.

```bash
Copy
dotnet            add            package
Microsoft.AspNetCore.SignalR
```

3. **Create the SignalR Hub**: In the **Hubs** folder, create a ChatHub class:

```
csharp
Copy
using Microsoft.AspNetCore.SignalR;

public class ChatHub : Hub
{
    public async Task SendMessage(string
user, string message)
    {
        await
Clients.All.SendAsync("ReceiveMessage",
user, message);
    }
}
```

Step 2: Set Up the Client Side (Views)

1. **Create the Chat View**
   (`Views/Home/Index.cshtml`): In the `Index` view,
   add the HTML structure for the chat interface and
   JavaScript code to interact with the SignalR hub.

```html
html
Copy
@{
    ViewData["Title"] = "Real-Time Chat";
}

<h2>@ViewData["Title"]</h2>

<div>
    <label for="user">Name:</label>
    <input type="text" id="user" />
</div>
<div>
    <label for="message">Message:</label>
    <input type="text" id="message" />
    <button
onclick="sendMessage()">Send</button>
</div>

<ul id="messagesList"></ul>
```

```
<script
src="https://cdn.jsdelivr.net/npm/@micros
oft/signalr@5.0.7/dist/browser/signalr.js
"></script>
<script>
    const      connection    =      new
signalR.HubConnectionBuilder()
        .withUrl("/chathub")
        .build();

    connection.start().catch(err        =>
console.error(err));

    connection.on("ReceiveMessage", (user,
message) => {
        const msg = `${user}: ${message}`;
        const          li            =
document.createElement("li");
        li.textContent = msg;

document.getElementById("messagesList").a
ppendChild(li);
    });

    function sendMessage() {
        const          user          =
document.getElementById("user").value;
        const         message         =
document.getElementById("message").value;
        connection.invoke("SendMessage",
user,        message).catch(err        =>
console.error(err));
    }
</script>
```

- o **Explanation**: This view provides an input field for the user's name, an input field for the message, and a button to send the message. Messages are displayed in an unordered list.

Step 3: Configure SignalR in Startup.cs

In the `ConfigureServices` method, add SignalR to the services collection. Then, in the `Configure` method, map the SignalR Hub route.

```csharp
Copy
public void ConfigureServices(IServiceCollection services)
{
    services.AddSignalR();
}

public void Configure(IApplicationBuilder app, IWebHostEnvironment env)
{
    app.UseRouting();

    app.UseEndpoints(endpoints =>
    {
        endpoints.MapHub<ChatHub>("/chathub");
        endpoints.MapControllerRoute(
            name: "default",
            pattern: "{controller=Home}/{action=Index}/{id?}");
    });
}
```

- **Explanation**: The SignalR `ChatHub` is mapped to the `/chathub` URL, and the main controller route is configured.

Step 4: Run the Application

After setting up the SignalR Hub and the client-side interactions, you can run the application using Visual Studio or the .NET CLI:

```
bash
Copy
dotnet run
```

Navigate to `http://localhost:5000/` to test the real-time chat application. Open the application in multiple browsers or tabs to simulate multiple users sending messages.

Best Practices for Real-Time Communication with SignalR

1. **Manage Connections Efficiently**: SignalR automatically handles connection management, but in complex applications, you may need to manage groups of users or implement features like private messaging.
2. **Handle Connection Lifecycle Events**: Use `OnConnectedAsync`, `OnDisconnectedAsync`, and other lifecycle events to handle logic like notifying users when someone joins or leaves the chat.
3. **Optimize Performance**: SignalR can handle thousands of concurrent connections, but it's essential to monitor performance and scale your application (e.g., by using Redis for SignalR backplane when running multiple servers).
4. **Security**: Always validate user input, use HTTPS for secure communication, and ensure that sensitive data is protected when sending messages.
5. **Error Handling**: Make sure to handle errors properly, both on the server and client side, to ensure a smooth user experience in case of network issues or unexpected events.

This chapter introduced **SignalR** and how to use it to implement real-time communication in web applications. We built a **real-time chat application** that allows users to send messages and receive instant updates.

CHAPTER TWENTY

Working with File Systems and Data Serialization

Reading and Writing Files in C#

In C#, you can easily interact with the file system using classes from the **System.IO** namespace. This allows you to read and write text and binary files, as well as manage directories and paths.

1. Writing to a File

To write data to a file in C#, you can use the `StreamWriter` class or the `File.WriteAllText` method for simpler cases.

Example: Writing to a Text File using `StreamWriter`:

```csharp
Copy
using System;
using System.IO;

public class FileWriter
{
    public void WriteToFile(string filePath,
string content)
    {
        using (StreamWriter writer = new
StreamWriter(filePath))
        {
            writer.WriteLine(content);
        }
```

```
        Console.WriteLine("File          written
successfully!");
    }
}
```

- **Explanation**: The StreamWriter is used to write text data to a file. The using statement ensures the file is properly closed after the write operation.

Example: Writing to a Text File using File.WriteAllText:

```csharp
csharp
Copy
using System;
using System.IO;

public class FileWriter
{
    public void WriteToFile(string filePath,
string content)
    {
        File.WriteAllText(filePath, content);
        Console.WriteLine("File          written
successfully!");
    }
}
```

- **Explanation**: File.WriteAllText is a shorthand method for writing a string to a file. It is simpler for cases where you don't need to manage the file stream manually.

2. Reading from a File

To read data from a file, you can use the StreamReader class or the File.ReadAllText method.

Example: Reading from a Text File using StreamReader:

199

```csharp
Copy
using System;
using System.IO;

public class FileReader
{
    public string ReadFromFile(string filePath)
    {
        using (StreamReader reader = new
StreamReader(filePath))
        {
            string content = reader.ReadToEnd();
            return content;
        }
    }
}
```

- **Explanation**: The StreamReader is used to read all the content from a file. The using statement ensures the file is properly closed after reading.

Example: Reading from a Text File using File.ReadAllText:

```csharp
Copy
using System;
using System.IO;

public class FileReader
{
    public string ReadFromFile(string filePath)
    {
        return File.ReadAllText(filePath);
    }
}
```

- **Explanation**: File.ReadAllText reads the entire content of the file into a string in one operation.

3. Handling File Paths

When working with file paths, use the `Path` class to manipulate file and directory paths safely.

Example: Combining Paths using `Path.Combine`:

```csharp
Copy
using System;
using System.IO;

public class FileHandler
{
    public string CombinePaths(string folderPath, string fileName)
    {
        return Path.Combine(folderPath, fileName);
    }
}
```

- **Explanation**: `Path.Combine` combines a folder path and a file name into a single valid path.

JSON and XML Serialization

Serialization is the process of converting an object into a format that can be easily stored or transmitted (such as JSON or XML). In C#, you can use built-in libraries like `System.Text.Json` for JSON serialization or `System.Xml.Serialization` for XML serialization.

1. JSON Serialization

JSON (JavaScript Object Notation) is a lightweight, human-readable format commonly used for data interchange. The .NET Core framework provides the `System.Text.Json` namespace for JSON serialization.

Example: Serializing an Object to JSON:

```csharp
Copy
using System;
using System.Text.Json;

public class Person
{
    public string Name { get; set; }
    public int Age { get; set; }
}

public class JsonSerializationExample
{
    public string SerializeToJson(Person person)
    {
        return JsonSerializer.Serialize(person);
    }
}
```

- **Explanation**: The `JsonSerializer.Serialize` method converts the `Person` object into a JSON string.

Example: Deserializing JSON to an Object:

```csharp
Copy
using System;
using System.Text.Json;

public class JsonDeserializationExample
{
```

202

```
    public   Person   DeserializeFromJson(string
jsonString)
    {
        return
JsonSerializer.Deserialize<Person>(jsonString);
    }
}
```

- **Explanation**: The `JsonSerializer.Deserialize` method converts a JSON string back into a `Person` object.

2. XML Serialization

XML (eXtensible Markup Language) is another format commonly used for data exchange. The .NET Core framework supports XML serialization via the `System.Xml.Serialization` namespace.

Example: Serializing an Object to XML:

```csharp
csharp
Copy
using System;
using System.IO;
using System.Xml.Serialization;

public class Person
{
    public string Name { get; set; }
    public int Age { get; set; }
}

public class XmlSerializationExample
{
    public void SerializeToXml(Person person,
string filePath)
    {
        var       serializer       =       new
XmlSerializer(typeof(Person));
```

203

```
        using       (var    writer    =    new
StreamWriter(filePath))
        {
            serializer.Serialize(writer,
person);
        }
    }
}
```

- **Explanation**: The `XmlSerializer.Serialize` method is used to serialize a `Person` object into XML and write it to a file.

Example: Deserializing XML to an Object:

```csharp
Copy
using System;
using System.IO;
using System.Xml.Serialization;

public class XmlDeserializationExample
{
    public    Person    DeserializeFromXml(string
filePath)
    {
        var        serializer      =       new
XmlSerializer(typeof(Person));
        using       (var    reader    =    new
StreamReader(filePath))
        {
            return
(Person)serializer.Deserialize(reader);
        }
    }
}
```

- **Explanation**: The `XmlSerializer.Deserialize` method reads XML from a file and converts it back into a `Person` object.

Real-World Example: Building a File Uploader with Serialization for Storing Data

Let's create a simple file uploader application that allows users to upload files, and the server will store the uploaded file data in JSON format for persistence. This application will involve both file handling and data serialization.

Step 1: Define the File Model

The file data model includes information about the file, such as the file name, size, and upload date.

```csharp
Copy
public class UploadedFile
{
    public string FileName { get; set; }
    public long FileSize { get; set; }
    public DateTime UploadDate { get; set; }
}
```

Step 2: Create the File Upload Logic

We will create an API endpoint for uploading files and store the metadata of each file in a JSON file.

```csharp
Copy
using Microsoft.AspNetCore.Http;
using Microsoft.AspNetCore.Mvc;
using System.IO;
using System.Text.Json;
using System.Threading.Tasks;

public class FileUploadController : Controller
{
```

```csharp
    private const string FileMetadataPath =
"fileMetadata.json";

    [HttpPost("upload")]
    public      async      Task<IActionResult>
UploadFile(IFormFile file)
    {
        // Save the file to the server
        var filePath = Path.Combine("uploads",
file.FileName);
        using    (var    stream    =    new
FileStream(filePath, FileMode.Create))
        {
            await file.CopyToAsync(stream);
        }

        // Create file metadata
        var fileMetadata = new UploadedFile
        {
            FileName = file.FileName,
            FileSize = file.Length,
            UploadDate = DateTime.Now
        };

        // Serialize metadata to JSON and save it
        SaveFileMetadata(fileMetadata);

        return Ok(new { message = "File uploaded
successfully!" });
    }

    private void SaveFileMetadata(UploadedFile
fileMetadata)
    {
        var    metadataList    =    new
List<UploadedFile>();

        // Check if metadata file exists and load
it
        if
(System.IO.File.Exists(FileMetadataPath))
        {
```

```
        var          existingJson      =
System.IO.File.ReadAllText(FileMetadataPath);
        metadataList               =
JsonSerializer.Deserialize<List<UploadedFile>>(
existingJson) ?? new List<UploadedFile>();
    }

    // Add new metadata
    metadataList.Add(fileMetadata);

    // Save the updated metadata to the JSON
file
    var             json           =
JsonSerializer.Serialize(metadataList,      new
JsonSerializerOptions { WriteIndented = true });

System.IO.File.WriteAllText(FileMetadataPath,
json);
    }
}
```

- **Explanation**:
  - The UploadFile action handles the file upload and saves the file to the uploads directory on the server.
  - The SaveFileMetadata method serializes the uploaded file metadata (file name, size, upload date) and stores it in a JSON file called fileMetadata.json.

Step 3: Create the Frontend (HTML Form)

Create a simple HTML form for uploading files:

```html
Copy
<form       action="/upload"       method="post"
enctype="multipart/form-data">
    <label     for="file">Choose     file    to
upload:</label>
```

```
    <input   type="file"   id="file"   name="file"
required />
    <button type="submit">Upload</button>
</form>
```

- **Explanation**: The HTML form allows users to choose a file and submit it to the server for uploading.

Best Practices for Working with File Systems and Serialization

1. **Validate File Input**: Always validate uploaded files (e.g., check file type, size) before processing them to prevent security issues.
2. **Error Handling**: Implement proper error handling for file upload failures, such as when the file exceeds the size limit or when the file cannot be written to the disk.
3. **Use Asynchronous I/O**: For better performance, especially with large files, use asynchronous file operations (`CopyToAsync`, `ReadAllTextAsync`, etc.).
4. **Avoid Storing Large Files in Memory**: When handling large files, avoid loading the entire file into memory. Instead, use streams to process the file in chunks.
5. **Security**: Ensure that uploaded files are stored in a secure location and that their names do not conflict with system files. You may also want to restrict certain file types for security reasons.

This chapter covered how to work with **file systems** in C# for reading and writing files and introduced **data serialization** using **JSON** and **XML**. We then built a **real-world file uploader application** with serialization to store file metadata.

CHAPTER TWENTYONE

Managing Application Configuration and Settings

Centralized Configuration Management

Configuration management is crucial for controlling and customizing application settings. It allows you to configure an application's behavior without changing the source code. Centralized configuration management ensures that configuration settings are managed in one place, making it easier to maintain and update.

What is Centralized Configuration Management?

- Centralized configuration management refers to the practice of storing and managing configuration settings in a single location that can be accessed by multiple instances of an application across different environments (e.g., development, testing, production).
- The goal is to ensure consistency, security, and ease of updating configuration settings across all services and environments.

Why Centralized Configuration Management?

- **Consistency**: Avoids discrepancies between environments by having a single source of truth for configuration.
- **Security**: Sensitive information (e.g., API keys, passwords) can be stored securely in a centralized system.

- **Scalability**: Makes it easier to scale applications when configuration settings are managed centrally, especially in microservice architectures.

In .NET, configuration management can be centralized using **Azure App Configuration** or **AWS Systems Manager Parameter Store**, but it is often handled with **appsettings.json** and environment variables, particularly in smaller applications or during development.

Environment Variables and AppSettings

In ASP.NET Core, there are several ways to manage configuration settings, including **appsettings.json**, **environment variables**, and **command-line arguments**.

1. Using `appsettings.json` for Configuration

`appsettings.json` is a popular choice for storing configuration settings in a simple, structured format. It is often used for settings that do not change between environments, such as application-specific parameters or static data.

Example: `appsettings.json`:

```json
Copy
{
  "AppSettings": {
    "ApplicationName": "MyApp",
    "MaxItems": 100,
    "EnableFeatureX": true
  },
  "ConnectionStrings": {
```

```
    "DefaultConnection":
"Server=myserver;Database=mydb;User=myuser;Pass
word=mypassword;"
    }
}
```

- **Explanation**: The `appsettings.json` file contains key-value pairs for general settings (`AppSettings`) and database connection strings (`ConnectionStrings`).

2. Using `appsettings.{Environment}.json` for Environment-Specific Settings

ASP.NET Core supports environment-specific configuration files like `appsettings.Development.json` or `appsettings.Production.json`. These files override settings in `appsettings.json` based on the environment the application is running in.

Example: `appsettings.Development.json`:

```json
Copy
{
  "AppSettings": {
    "MaxItems": 200
  },
  "ConnectionStrings": {
    "DefaultConnection":
"Server=devserver;Database=devdb;User=devuser;P
assword=devpassword;"
  }
}
```

- **Explanation**: The `appsettings.Development.json` file contains environment-specific overrides. These settings will be used if the application is running in the `Development` environment.

3. Environment Variables for Configuration

Environment variables provide a way to store sensitive or environment-specific configuration settings outside of the application's code or configuration files. They are especially useful in production environments where it is important not to store sensitive data in code or config files.

Example: Setting Environment Variables:

```bash
Copy
SET MyApp__AppSettings__ApplicationName=MyAppProd
SET MyApp__ConnectionStrings__DefaultConnection=Server=prodserver;Database=proddb;User=produser;Password=prodpassword;
```

- **Explanation**: Environment variables use a double underscore (__) to represent nested properties, such as `AppSettings:ApplicationName` in `appsettings.json`.

4. Accessing Configuration in C#

To access configuration values in ASP.NET Core, you use the `IConfiguration` service, which is automatically available via dependency injection.

Example: Accessing Configuration in a Controller:

```csharp
Copy
using Microsoft.AspNetCore.Mvc;
using Microsoft.Extensions.Configuration;

public class HomeController : Controller
```

212

```csharp
{
    private readonly IConfiguration
_configuration;

    public HomeController(IConfiguration
configuration)
    {
        _configuration = configuration;
    }

    public IActionResult Index()
    {
        var appName =
_configuration["AppSettings:ApplicationName"];
        var maxItems =
_configuration.GetValue<int>("AppSettings:MaxIt
ems");
        var connectionString =
_configuration.GetConnectionString("DefaultConn
ection");

        ViewBag.AppName = appName;
        ViewBag.MaxItems = maxItems;
        ViewBag.ConnectionString =
connectionString;

        return View();
    }
}
```

- **Explanation**: The IConfiguration service is injected into the controller, allowing you to access values from appsettings.json or environment variables. You can use GetValue<T> to retrieve typed values or GetConnectionString to retrieve connection strings.

Real-World Example: Configuring a Multi-Environment Application

In this example, we'll create a simple **ASP.NET Core web application** that is configured for multiple environments (Development, Staging, and Production). We will use `appsettings.json`, `appsettings.{Environment}.json`, and environment variables to configure the application.

Step 1: Set Up Configuration Files

1. **appsettings.json**:

```json
Copy
{
  "AppSettings": {
    "ApplicationName": "MyApp",
    "MaxItems": 50
  },
  "ConnectionStrings": {
    "DefaultConnection":
"Server=myserver;Database=mydb;User=myuser;Pass
word=mypassword;"
  }
}
```

2. **appsettings.Development.json**:

```json
Copy
{
  "AppSettings": {
    "MaxItems": 100
  },
  "ConnectionStrings": {
    "DefaultConnection":
"Server=devserver;Database=devdb;User=devuser;P
assword=devpassword;"
  }
}
```

3. **appsettings.Production.json**:

```json
Copy
{
  "AppSettings": {
    "MaxItems": 200
  },
  "ConnectionStrings": {
    "DefaultConnection":
"Server=prodserver;Database=proddb;User=produse
r;Password=prodpassword;"
  }
}
```

Step 2: Configure the Environment in Startup.cs

In the `ConfigureServices` method of `Startup.cs`, ensure that the configuration is set up to load the appropriate environment-specific settings:

```csharp
Copy
public void ConfigureServices(IServiceCollection
services)
{
    services.AddControllersWithViews();

    // Load configuration settings based on
environment
    var             environment             =
Environment.GetEnvironmentVariable("ASPNETCORE_
ENVIRONMENT");
    Console.WriteLine($"Current      Environment:
{environment}");
}
```

- **Explanation**: The environment is set automatically by ASP.NET Core based on the hosting environment (e.g., Development, Staging, Production). The environment variable ASPNETCORE_ENVIRONMENT determines which `appsettings.{Environment}.json` file will be loaded.

Step 3: Configure Environment Variables

For **Production** settings, store sensitive data like database connection strings in environment variables rather than in `appsettings.json`. For example:

```bash
Copy
SET ASPNETCORE_ENVIRONMENT=Production
SET MyApp__AppSettings__MaxItems=300
SET
MyApp__ConnectionStrings__DefaultConnection=Ser
ver=prodserver;Database=proddb;User=produser;Pa
ssword=prodpassword;
```

- **Explanation**: Here, `MyApp__AppSettings__MaxItems` and the connection string are set via environment variables, and they will override the corresponding values in `appsettings.Production.json`.

Step 4: Access Configuration in Your Application

You can now access these configuration values in your application just as you would with the default configuration:

```csharp
Copy
public class HomeController : Controller
{
    private      readonly       IConfiguration
_configuration;

    public       HomeController(IConfiguration
configuration)
    {
```

```
    _configuration = configuration;
}

public IActionResult Index()
{
    var            appName            =
_configuration["AppSettings:ApplicationName"];
    var            maxItems           =
_configuration.GetValue<int>("AppSettings:MaxIt
ems");
    var         connectionString       =
_configuration.GetConnectionString("DefaultConn
ection");

    ViewBag.AppName = appName;
    ViewBag.MaxItems = maxItems;
    ViewBag.ConnectionString            =
connectionString;

    return View();
}
}
```

- **Explanation**: The configuration system in ASP.NET Core automatically resolves the correct settings based on the environment and any environment variables set, making it easy to manage different environments.

Best Practices for Managing Configuration and Settings

1. **Separate Configuration by Environment**: Use environment-specific configuration files (appsettings.{Environment}.json) to keep settings consistent across different environments while allowing for environment-specific overrides.

2. **Use Environment Variables for Sensitive Data**: Store sensitive information such as API keys, passwords, and connection strings in environment

variables or secure vaults, not in `appsettings.json`.

3. **Use Strongly Typed Configuration**: Consider binding your configuration settings to strongly typed classes using `IOptions<T>` for better validation, IntelliSense support, and easier access to settings.

4. **Centralized Configuration Management**: For large applications or microservices, use centralized configuration management tools like **Azure App Configuration** or **AWS Systems Manager Parameter Store** for a unified and secure configuration approach.

5. **Avoid Hardcoding Settings**: Always read configuration settings from files or environment variables rather than hardcoding them into the application.

This chapter covered **managing application configuration and settings** in C# using `appsettings.json`, environment variables, and centralized configuration techniques. We explored how to set up multi-environment configurations and provided a real-world example of a configuration system that adapts to different environments.

CHAPTER TWENTYTWO

Security Best Practices in Enterprise Applications

Common Security Threats

Security threats are one of the most critical concerns for any application, particularly in enterprise environments where sensitive data and critical business operations are involved. Some of the most common security threats include:

1. SQL Injection

SQL injection occurs when an attacker is able to insert or manipulate SQL queries by exploiting vulnerable input fields in an application. This can lead to unauthorized access to the database, data manipulation, or even complete database compromise.

2. Cross-Site Scripting (XSS)

XSS attacks occur when an attacker injects malicious scripts (usually JavaScript) into a webpage that is then executed by other users' browsers. This can lead to stolen session tokens, user impersonation, or even malicious actions being taken on behalf of the victim.

3. Cross-Site Request Forgery (CSRF)

CSRF attacks occur when a malicious actor tricks a user into performing actions on a web application in which they are authenticated, such as changing account settings or making a financial transaction.

4. Insecure Deserialization

Insecure deserialization happens when an application deserializes untrusted data, potentially leading to remote code execution, unauthorized access, or data corruption.

5. Broken Authentication and Session Management

This includes flaws in the authentication process that allow attackers to bypass login procedures, hijack sessions, or impersonate other users.

6. Sensitive Data Exposure

Sensitive data exposure occurs when sensitive information such as passwords, credit card details, or personal data is stored or transmitted insecurely.

7. Insufficient Logging and Monitoring

Without proper logging and monitoring, attackers can exploit vulnerabilities without being detected, making it difficult to prevent or mitigate future attacks.

Best Practices for Secure Coding

To secure your application against common threats, there are several **secure coding best practices** to follow:

1. SQL Injection Protection

SQL injection can be mitigated by using **parameterized queries** or **ORMs** (Object-Relational Mappers) like Entity Framework, which automatically generates secure SQL queries.

Best Practice: Always use parameterized queries or stored procedures to prevent SQL injection.

Example: Using Parameterized Queries in ADO.NET:

```csharp
Copy
using (var command = new SqlCommand("SELECT *
FROM Users WHERE Username = @username AND
Password = @password", connection))
{

command.Parameters.AddWithValue("@username",
username);

command.Parameters.AddWithValue("@password",
password);

    var reader = command.ExecuteReader();
    // Handle results
}
```

2. Cross-Site Scripting (XSS) Protection

XSS can be prevented by **escaping user input** before displaying it in the browser, ensuring that malicious code is not executed. Additionally, use HTTP-only cookies and Content Security Policy (CSP) headers.

Best Practice: Always encode output (e.g., HTML, JavaScript) to prevent execution of malicious scripts.

Example: Encoding Output in ASP.NET Core:

```csharp
Copy
@Html.Encode(userInput)
```
3. Cross-Site Request Forgery (CSRF) Protection

CSRF attacks can be prevented by using anti-CSRF tokens. ASP.NET Core automatically includes an anti-CSRF token in form submissions when using `@Html.AntiForgeryToken()` in your Razor views.

Best Practice: Always include anti-CSRF tokens in forms that perform state-changing operations.

Example: Adding an Anti-CSRF Token in ASP.NET Core:

```html
Copy
<form method="post">
    @Html.AntiForgeryToken()
    <!-- Form fields go here -->
    <button type="submit">Submit</button>
</form>
```

In the controller, validate the token:

```csharp
Copy
[HttpPost]
```

```
[ValidateAntiForgeryToken]
public IActionResult SubmitForm(DataModel model)
{
    // Handle the form submission
}
```

4. Insecure Deserialization Protection

To prevent insecure deserialization, avoid using untrusted data in serialization processes. Validate all incoming data and ensure that only safe objects are deserialized.

Best Practice: Use secure serialization techniques and avoid deserializing data from untrusted sources.

5. Broken Authentication and Session Management

Secure session management involves using secure, HttpOnly cookies for authentication tokens and ensuring that the session is invalidated upon logout. Use strong password policies and multi-factor authentication (MFA) to secure login processes.

Best Practice: Always use secure session cookies (Secure, HttpOnly), implement strong authentication mechanisms, and enforce session expiration.

Example: Secure Session Cookies in ASP.NET Core:

```csharp
Copy
services.AddAuthentication(CookieAuthentication
Defaults.AuthenticationScheme)
    .AddCookie(options =>
    {
        options.Cookie.SecurePolicy        =
CookieSecurePolicy.Always;
        options.Cookie.HttpOnly = true;
```

```
});
```

6. Sensitive Data Exposure Protection

Sensitive data should be encrypted both at rest and in transit. Use **TLS/SSL** for data transmitted over the network and encrypt sensitive data stored in databases or files using strong encryption algorithms.

Best Practice: Always use HTTPS (TLS) for sensitive communication and encrypt sensitive data.

Example: Forcing HTTPS in ASP.NET Core:

```csharp
Copy
public void Configure(IApplicationBuilder app)
{
    app.UseHttpsRedirection();
}
```

7. Logging and Monitoring

Always log important security events (e.g., failed login attempts, permission changes) and monitor these logs for suspicious activity. Ensure logs are stored securely and access is limited to authorized personnel.

Best Practice: Use logging frameworks like **Serilog** or **NLog** and integrate with cloud logging services for monitoring and alerting.

224

Real-World Example: Securing an Application against SQL Injection and Cross-Site Scripting

Let's consider an example of securing a simple application with both **SQL Injection** and **Cross-Site Scripting (XSS)** protections.

Step 1: Securing Against SQL Injection

In this example, we will create a login system where the username and password are validated against a database. To prevent SQL injection, we will use parameterized queries.

Controller Example:

```csharp
Copy
using System.Data.SqlClient;
using Microsoft.AspNetCore.Mvc;

public class AccountController : Controller
{
    private readonly string _connectionString =
"your_connection_string";

    public IActionResult Login(string username,
string password)
    {
        string query = "SELECT COUNT(*) FROM
Users WHERE Username = @username AND Password =
@password";

        using (var connection = new
SqlConnection(_connectionString))
        {
            var command = new SqlCommand(query,
connection);
```

```
command.Parameters.AddWithValue("@username",
username);

command.Parameters.AddWithValue("@password",
password);

            connection.Open();
            int             result         =
(int)command.ExecuteScalar();

            if (result > 0)
            {
                return
RedirectToAction("Welcome");
            }
            else
            {
                return
RedirectToAction("LoginFailed");
            }
        }
    }
}
```

- **Explanation**: By using `command.Parameters.AddWithValue`, we ensure that user input is treated as data, not executable code, preventing SQL injection attacks.

Step 2: Securing Against Cross-Site Scripting (XSS)

To prevent XSS, we will encode any user-generated content before rendering it in the browser. In ASP.NET Core, this is done automatically using the @Html or @ syntax for displaying variables in Razor views.

View Example (Razor):

```
html
```

```
Copy
@model MyApp.Models.UserInputModel

<h2>Your Input</h2>
<p>@Html.Encode(Model.UserInput)</p>
```

- **Explanation**: The `@Html.Encode()` method ensures that any special characters in user input (like <, >, and &) are escaped and rendered as text, not as HTML or JavaScript, preventing XSS attacks.

Step 3: Testing the Application

1. **Test SQL Injection Prevention**: Try submitting SQL injection payloads like `admin' OR '1'='1` to the login form. Since we're using parameterized queries, these attempts should not work.
2. **Test XSS Prevention**: Try submitting a script tag, such as `<script>alert('XSS')</script>`, and ensure it is displayed as text rather than executed.

Best Practices Summary for Security in Enterprise Applications

1. **Input Validation**: Always validate and sanitize user input to prevent malicious content from entering the system.
2. **Use Secure Frameworks and Libraries**: Use libraries like **Entity Framework** and **ASP.NET Core**'s built-in protections to avoid common security pitfalls like SQL injection and XSS.
3. **Encryption**: Encrypt sensitive data both in transit (using TLS) and at rest (using strong encryption algorithms).
4. **Authentication and Authorization**: Implement strong authentication methods (e.g., multi-factor authentication) and ensure role-based authorization to restrict access to sensitive data.

5. **Session Management**: Use secure cookies, manage session expiration, and implement proper session handling to protect against session hijacking.
6. **Regular Security Audits**: Conduct regular security audits and penetration testing to identify and fix vulnerabilities.
7. **Logging and Monitoring**: Implement logging and continuous monitoring to detect suspicious activities and respond to security incidents quickly.

This chapter covered **security best practices** in enterprise applications, including protections against **SQL injection** and **cross-site scripting (XSS)**. We discussed various common threats and provided examples of securing applications.

CHAPTER TWENTYTHREE

Building and Deploying Windows Applications

Introduction to Windows Forms and WPF

In the world of Windows development, two main frameworks are commonly used for building desktop applications: **Windows Forms (WinForms)** and **Windows Presentation Foundation (WPF)**. Both frameworks allow developers to create graphical user interfaces (GUIs) for Windows applications, but they offer different features and capabilities.

1. Windows Forms (WinForms)

Windows Forms is a UI framework for building traditional desktop applications. It has been around since .NET Framework 1.0 and is a good choice for building simple applications with relatively straightforward user interfaces. WinForms is primarily event-driven and uses controls like buttons, text boxes, and labels to create forms-based UIs.

Features of WinForms:

- Simple and easy to use for creating basic UI applications.
- Provides a wide range of standard controls (e.g., buttons, textboxes, labels).
- Lightweight and quick to develop for smaller applications.

When to Use WinForms:

- For quick and simple desktop applications.
- When you need compatibility with older Windows systems or want to leverage legacy code.

2. Windows Presentation Foundation (WPF)

WPF is a more modern UI framework introduced with .NET Framework 3.0. It is designed for building rich desktop applications with advanced graphics, animations, and sophisticated user interfaces. WPF uses XAML (eXtensible Application Markup Language) for defining the UI, which provides a declarative approach to designing complex layouts and controls.

Features of WPF:

- Supports advanced graphics and 3D rendering.
- Uses XAML for declarative UI design, which is more flexible than WinForms.
- Provides support for data binding, making it easier to bind UI elements to data sources.
- Includes powerful tools for styling and templating the UI using **Styles**, **Templates**, and **Control Templates**.
- Supports **MVVM** (Model-View-ViewModel) design pattern, which helps in separating the UI from the business logic.

When to Use WPF:

- For complex, feature-rich desktop applications.
- When you need advanced styling, animations, and graphics.
- When you need a modern UI with data-binding capabilities.

Real-World Example: Building a Desktop Accounting Software

In this section, we will build a simple **desktop accounting software** application using **WPF**. This application will allow users to:

- Add income and expenses.
- View a list of transactions.
- Calculate and display the balance.

We will demonstrate how to set up the application, create the UI, and implement basic functionality like adding transactions and calculating the balance.

Step 1: Create the WPF Project

Using Visual Studio, create a new **WPF App** project. You can do this by selecting the **WPF App (.NET Core)** template.

1. Open Visual Studio.
2. Click **Create a new project**.
3. Select **WPF App (.NET Core)** and click **Next**.
4. Name the project (e.g., `AccountingApp`) and choose a location.
5. Click **Create**.

This creates a basic WPF application with a default window (`MainWindow.xaml`).

Step 2: Define the Transaction Model

Define a model to represent a transaction in our accounting software. A transaction will have a type (income or expense), an amount, and a description.

```csharp
Copy
public class Transaction
{
    public string Type { get; set; }  // "Income"
or "Expense"
    public decimal Amount { get; set; }
    public string Description { get; set; }
}
```

Step 3: Design the UI

Open `MainWindow.xaml` and design the UI using XAML. The UI will include:

- A text box for the description of the transaction.
- A combo box to choose the transaction type (Income or Expense).
- A text box to enter the amount.
- A button to add the transaction.
- A list box to display the transactions.
- A label to show the current balance.

```xml
Copy
<Window x:Class="AccountingApp.MainWindow"

xmlns="http://schemas.microsoft.com/winfx/2006/
xaml/presentation"

xmlns:x="http://schemas.microsoft.com/winfx/200
6/xaml"
        Title="Accounting Software" Height="450"
Width="800">
```

```
<Grid>
    <TextBox        x:Name="DescriptionTextBox"
HorizontalAlignment="Left"    Margin="20,20,0,0"
VerticalAlignment="Top" Width="200" />
    <ComboBox           x:Name="TypeComboBox"
HorizontalAlignment="Left"    Margin="240,20,0,0"
VerticalAlignment="Top" Width="150">
        <ComboBoxItem Content="Income" />
        <ComboBoxItem Content="Expense" />
    </ComboBox>
    <TextBox          x:Name="AmountTextBox"
HorizontalAlignment="Left"    Margin="420,20,0,0"
VerticalAlignment="Top" Width="100" />
    <Button     Content="Add      Transaction"
HorizontalAlignment="Left"
VerticalAlignment="Top"  Width="120"  Height="30"
Margin="550,20,0,0"
Click="AddTransactionButton_Click" />

    <ListBox    x:Name="TransactionListBox"
HorizontalAlignment="Left"        Height="200"
Margin="20,60,0,0"      VerticalAlignment="Top"
Width="730" />

    <Label              x:Name="BalanceLabel"
Content="Balance:                      $0.00"
HorizontalAlignment="Left"
VerticalAlignment="Bottom"    Margin="20,0,0,20"
Width="200" Height="30"/>
    </Grid>
</Window>
```

- **Explanation**: We define the layout using a Grid with controls such as TextBox, ComboBox, Button, ListBox, and Label. Each control is given a name so it can be accessed in the code-behind.

Step 4: Implementing the Code-Behind

Now, in the `MainWindow.xaml.cs` file, implement the logic for adding transactions, calculating the balance, and displaying the transactions.

```csharp
Copy
using System.Collections.Generic;
using System.Windows;

namespace AccountingApp
{
    public partial class MainWindow : Window
    {
        private List<Transaction> transactions;
        private decimal balance;

        public MainWindow()
        {
            InitializeComponent();
            transactions = new
List<Transaction>();
            balance = 0;
        }

        private                          void
AddTransactionButton_Click(object         sender,
RoutedEventArgs e)
        {
            // Get input values
            string         description         =
DescriptionTextBox.Text;
            string            type            =
((ComboBoxItem)TypeComboBox.SelectedItem)?.Cont
ent.ToString();
            decimal amount;

            if
(string.IsNullOrEmpty(description)  ||  type  ==
null   ||   !decimal.TryParse(AmountTextBox.Text,
out amount))
```

234

```csharp
        {
            MessageBox.Show("Please fill all
fields correctly.");
            return;
        }

        // Create a new transaction
        var transaction = new Transaction
        {
            Description = description,
            Type = type,
            Amount = amount
        };

        // Add the transaction to the list
        transactions.Add(transaction);

        // Update the balance
        if (type == "Income")
        {
            balance += amount;
        }
        else if (type == "Expense")
        {
            balance -= amount;
        }

        // Update the UI
TransactionListBox.Items.Add($"{transaction.Typ
e}:        {transaction.Description}        -
${transaction.Amount}");
        BalanceLabel.Content   =   $"Balance:
${balance:F2}";

        // Clear input fields
        DescriptionTextBox.Clear();
        AmountTextBox.Clear();
        }
    }
}
```

- **Explanation**:

235

- o **AddTransactionButton_Click** handles the button click event.
- o It validates the inputs, creates a new transaction object, and adds it to the transaction list.
- o It updates the balance based on whether the transaction is an income or an expense.
- o The transaction is displayed in the ListBox, and the balance is updated on the UI.

Step 5: Running the Application

Once the application is built, you can run it in Visual Studio. When you add transactions, the list of transactions will update, and the balance will reflect the income and expenses in real-time.

Best Practices for Building Windows Applications

1. **Separation of Concerns (MVC or MVVM)**: Use patterns like **MVVM (Model-View-ViewModel)** to separate the UI logic from the business logic and ensure maintainability.
2. **Data Binding**: In WPF, use **data binding** to automatically update the UI when data changes. This reduces the amount of code required for UI updates.
3. **Error Handling**: Always implement error handling for user input and unexpected application failures (e.g., invalid data, failed file writes).
4. **Validation**: Validate user input before performing operations like database writes or calculations. Use custom validation for user forms.
5. **Performance Optimization**: For complex applications, optimize performance by using async operations and ensuring that heavy calculations do not block the UI thread.

This chapter introduced **Windows Forms** and **WPF** as frameworks for building desktop applications and walked through a real-world example of **building a desktop accounting software**. We covered how to design the UI using XAML, handle user input in the code-behind, and display results dynamically. Would you like to explore more advanced topics such as **data-binding**, **MVVM pattern**, or **deploying desktop applications**?

CHAPTER TWENTYFOUR

Continuous Integration and Continuous Delivery (CI/CD) in C#

What Is CI/CD?

CI/CD stands for **Continuous Integration** and **Continuous Delivery/Continuous Deployment**, and it is a set of practices and methodologies used to automate and streamline the process of software development, testing, and deployment.

1. Continuous Integration (CI)

Continuous Integration is the practice of frequently integrating code changes from multiple contributors into a shared repository. The key idea is to run automated tests and build processes each time changes are made to ensure that code merges smoothly, doesn't introduce bugs, and is always ready for deployment.

Benefits of CI:

- **Frequent Testing**: Automated tests run after each integration, catching bugs and issues early.
- **Faster Feedback**: Developers receive immediate feedback if their code breaks the build or causes test failures.
- **Improved Code Quality**: With frequent integration, integration issues are detected and addressed early, leading to fewer conflicts.

2. Continuous Delivery (CD)

Continuous Delivery extends CI by automating the process of preparing code for release. It ensures that the code is always in a deployable state. This means that after every change, the application can be automatically deployed to a staging or testing environment, where it can be validated.

3. Continuous Deployment

Continuous Deployment takes CD one step further by automating the actual deployment of code changes to production. With this approach, every change that passes through the CI/CD pipeline is automatically deployed to production, making new features and fixes available to users as soon as they are ready.

Benefits of CD:

- **Faster Time to Market**: Code is always ready for release, meaning new features and bug fixes can be shipped to users quickly.
- **Reduced Risk of Errors**: By automating deployments, human errors in the deployment process are minimized.
- **Easier Rollback**: With CI/CD, version control is integrated into the process, making it easier to roll back to previous versions in case of failure.

Setting Up a CI/CD Pipeline

A **CI/CD pipeline** automates the entire process of building, testing, and deploying software. Setting up a CI/CD pipeline for a C# application typically involves using services like **Azure DevOps**, **GitHub Actions**, or **Jenkins**.

1. Choose a CI/CD Service

There are several tools and platforms available for setting up CI/CD pipelines. Some of the most popular choices for C# development are:

- **Azure DevOps**: A suite of DevOps tools provided by Microsoft, including build, release, and testing tools.
- **GitHub Actions**: A feature of GitHub that automates software workflows for CI/CD.
- **Jenkins**: An open-source automation server that helps automate parts of the software development process.
- **CircleCI**: A cloud-native CI/CD tool designed to automate testing and deployment.

2. Configure a Build Pipeline

A build pipeline automatically builds and tests your application when changes are committed to the repository. Here is how you would configure a basic **Azure DevOps** build pipeline for a C# project.

1. **Create a New Pipeline**: In **Azure DevOps**, navigate to your project and select **Pipelines → New Pipeline**.
2. **Choose Your Repository**: Select the repository that contains your C# application (e.g., GitHub, Azure Repos).
3. **Select Build Template**: For a C# project, you can select the **.NET Core** template, which provides a default pipeline for building and testing C# applications.
4. **Configure Build Steps**: The build steps may look like this in `azure-pipelines.yml`:

```yaml
Copy
trigger:
- main
```

```
pool:
  vmImage: 'windows-latest'

steps:
- task: UseDotNet@2
  inputs:
    packageType: 'sdk'
    version: '5.x'
    installationPath:
$(Agent.ToolsDirectory)/dotnet

- task: DotNetCoreCLI@2
  inputs:
    command: 'restore'
    projects: '**/*.csproj'

- task: DotNetCoreCLI@2
  inputs:
    command: 'build'
    projects: '**/*.csproj'

- task: DotNetCoreCLI@2
  inputs:
    command: 'test'
    projects: '**/*.csproj'

- task: DotNetCoreCLI@2
  inputs:
    command: 'publish'
    projects: '**/*.csproj'
    publishWebProjects: false
    zipAfterPublish: true
    artifactName: 'drop'
```

- **Explanation**:
    - o The `trigger` defines the branch (`main`) that will trigger the pipeline.
    - o The `UseDotNet` task ensures the correct .NET SDK is installed.
    - o The `DotNetCoreCLI` tasks restore, build, test, and publish the application.

3. Set Up a Release Pipeline

After the build pipeline successfully runs, the next step is the **release pipeline**, which automates the deployment process to staging or production environments.

1. **Create a Release Pipeline**: In **Azure DevOps**, navigate to **Pipelines** → **Releases** → **New Pipeline**.
2. **Add an Artifact**: Link the build artifact produced by the build pipeline to the release pipeline.
3. **Configure Deployment**: Set up environments for deploying the application (e.g., development, staging, production). You can add tasks like:
   o Deploy to **Azure App Services**, **AWS**, or any other hosting environment.
   o Perform smoke tests, validation, or approval steps.
4. **Automate the Deployment**: Once everything is configured, your pipeline will automatically deploy to the target environment each time the build completes.

Real-World Example: Automating Deployment for an Enterprise Application

Let's create a simple **C# web application** for an enterprise environment, and set up a CI/CD pipeline to automate the process of building, testing, and deploying the application.

Step 1: Build the Application

1. Create a simple **ASP.NET Core** web application using the following steps:
   o In Visual Studio or using the .NET CLI, create a new ASP.NET Core Web API project:

```
bash
Copy
dotnet new webapi -n EnterpriseApp
```

- o Implement basic controllers, services, and models (this could be any functionality your application requires).

2. Add unit tests for the application to ensure quality. These tests will be run in the CI pipeline.

Step 2: Set Up the CI Pipeline

1. **Create a Build Pipeline in Azure DevOps**:
   - o Navigate to Azure DevOps and create a new pipeline.
   - o Use the .NET Core template to set up a pipeline that builds, restores, and tests the project.
   - o Add tasks for restoring NuGet packages, building the project, and running unit tests (like in the earlier azure-pipelines.yml example).

2. **Add Code Coverage and Tests**: To ensure that your application is well-tested, you can add a task to check for code coverage.

   Example in azure-pipelines.yml:

```
yaml
Copy
- task: PublishTestResults@2
  inputs:
     testResultsFormat: 'JUnit'
     testResultsFiles:
'**/TestResults/*.xml'
     failTaskOnFailedTests: true
```

Step 3: Set Up the Release Pipeline

1. **Create a Release Pipeline**:

- o Add a new release pipeline that will deploy the web application to **Azure App Services**.
- o Link the build artifact from the build pipeline to the release pipeline.

2. **Define Environments**:
   - o Set up environments such as **Development**, **Staging**, and **Production**.
   - o Each environment can have its own set of deployment tasks (e.g., for Azure, you can use the **Azure Web App Deploy** task).

3. **Deploy to Staging**:
   - o Set the staging environment to deploy automatically after a successful build.
   - o Configure approval gates, if necessary, to control when code should move to the production environment.

4. **Deploy to Production**:
   - o In the production environment, configure deployment to trigger after the staging environment is validated.
   - o You can set up manual approval steps for production deployment or deploy automatically depending on the release process.

Step 4: Monitor and Maintain the Pipeline

1. **Monitoring**:
   - o Azure DevOps provides monitoring and logging tools for pipelines. You can check for build failures, deployment issues, and test results.
   - o Use dashboards in Azure DevOps to visualize pipeline success rates, build times, and deployment health.

2. **Updating the Pipeline**:
   - o As your application evolves, you can update the pipeline to include new tasks, tools, or deployment targets. For example, if you add new

services, modify the `azure-pipelines.yml` to accommodate the new build or deployment steps.

Best Practices for CI/CD in C#

1. **Automate Testing**: Ensure that your CI pipeline includes automated unit tests and integration tests. This helps catch bugs early and improves the quality of the code.
2. **Use Versioning**: Implement versioning strategies for your artifacts and deployments to keep track of different releases.
3. **Secure Secrets**: Store sensitive information (e.g., API keys, credentials) in a secure environment like **Azure Key Vault** or **AWS Secrets Manager**, and reference them in your CI/CD pipeline.
4. **Incremental Builds**: Optimize your build process by using incremental builds to save time and resources.
5. **Rollback Strategy**: Have a rollback plan in place in case a deployment fails. Implement mechanisms like blue/green deployments or canary releases to ensure minimal downtime.
6. **Monitor Production**: Continuously monitor the production environment to detect any issues that might arise from recent deployments.

This chapter covered **Continuous Integration** and **Continuous Delivery (CI/CD)**, explaining the key concepts and steps to automate the build, testing, and deployment of a C# application. We walked through the process of setting up a CI/CD pipeline and provided a real-world example of automating deployment for an enterprise application.

CHAPTER TWENTYFIVE

Monitoring and Logging for Enterprise Applications

Monitoring and **logging** are essential practices for any application, particularly in enterprise environments. These practices help maintain the health and performance of applications, detect issues, and ensure the application runs smoothly in production.

1. Monitoring

Monitoring involves tracking the performance, availability, and health of an application or system. It allows you to detect problems in real-time and take corrective action before they impact users. Monitoring can be done for:

- **Application performance**: CPU, memory usage, response times, etc.
- **Availability**: Ensuring the system is accessible and functioning as expected.
- **Business metrics**: Tracking application-specific metrics such as transaction success rates, user activity, etc.

Benefits of Monitoring:

- **Early Detection of Issues**: Identifies problems before they affect users, such as performance degradation or system outages.

- **Proactive Problem Solving**: Enables faster detection and resolution of issues through alerts, reducing downtime.
- **Performance Optimization**: Provides insight into system bottlenecks or inefficiencies.

2. Logging

Logging involves capturing detailed information about an application's runtime behavior, events, and errors. Logs provide a historical record of what happened in the system, making it easier to investigate issues and understand system behavior.

Types of Logs:

- **Error Logs**: Capture exceptions or failures in the system.
- **Info Logs**: Track significant events or system milestones (e.g., user login, transaction completed).
- **Debug Logs**: Provide detailed insights into the system's internal workings (e.g., function calls, variable values) for troubleshooting.

Benefits of Logging:

- **Error Diagnosis**: Helps diagnose issues by providing detailed information about what happened before an error occurred.
- **Audit Trails**: Provides an audit trail of user actions and system events, useful for security and compliance.
- **Performance Analysis**: Logs can help analyze application performance and identify bottlenecks.

3. Combining Monitoring and Logging

While **monitoring** provides real-time insights into the system's health and performance, **logging** offers detailed

247

information for diagnosing and investigating issues after the fact. Combining both tools is key to achieving comprehensive observability.

Using Serilog, NLog, and Application Insights

Several tools and libraries are available for implementing logging and monitoring in enterprise applications. In this section, we'll cover three popular tools:

1. Serilog

Serilog is a simple yet powerful logging library for .NET. It allows structured logging, making it easy to integrate with different sinks (e.g., file, database, cloud services) for storing log data.

Setting Up Serilog:

1. Install the Serilog NuGet packages:

    ```bash
    bash
    Copy
    dotnet add package Serilog
    dotnet add package Serilog.Sinks.Console
    dotnet add package Serilog.Sinks.File
    ```

2. Configure Serilog in your `Program.cs`:

    ```csharp
    csharp
    Copy
    using Serilog;

    public class Program
    {
    ```

```
public static void Main(string[] args)
{
    Log.Logger              =              new
LoggerConfiguration()
        .WriteTo.Console()

.WriteTo.File("logs\\log.txt",
rollingInterval: RollingInterval.Day)
        .CreateLogger();

    try
    {
        Log.Information("Application
Starting...");

CreateHostBuilder(args).Build().Run();
    }
    catch (Exception ex)
    {
        Log.Fatal(ex,      "Application
failed to start");
    }
    finally
    {
        Log.CloseAndFlush();
    }
}

public      static      IHostBuilder
CreateHostBuilder(string[] args) =>
    Host.CreateDefaultBuilder(args)

.ConfigureWebHostDefaults(webBuilder =>
        {

webBuilder.UseStartup<Startup>();
        });
}
```

3. Log information, warnings, and errors throughout your application:

```
csharp
Copy
Log.Information("Processing    payment    for
user {UserId}", userId);
Log.Warning("Failed to process payment for
user {UserId}", userId);
Log.Error(ex,  "Error   processing   payment
for user {UserId}", userId);
```

- **Explanation**: Serilog allows you to configure different sinks for logging output, such as the console or a log file. It also supports structured logging, which makes querying and analyzing logs easier.

2. NLog

NLog is another popular logging framework for .NET, offering rich features like logging to multiple targets (file, database, email) and configurable logging rules.

Setting Up NLog:

1. Install the NLog NuGet packages:

```
bash
Copy
dotnet add package NLog
dotnet add package NLog.Web.AspNetCore
```

2. Configure NLog in your `Program.cs`:

```
csharp
Copy
using NLog;
using NLog.Web;

public class Program
{
    public static void Main(string[] args)
```

```csharp
        {

LogManager.LoadConfiguration("nlog.config
");
        var            logger            =
LogManager.GetCurrentClassLogger();
        try
        {
            logger.Info("Application
Starting...");

CreateHostBuilder(args).Build().Run();
        }
        catch (Exception ex)
        {
            logger.Error(ex,   "Application
failed to start");
            throw;
        }
        finally
        {
            LogManager.Shutdown();
        }
    }

    public        static        IHostBuilder
CreateHostBuilder(string[] args) =>
        Host.CreateDefaultBuilder(args)

.ConfigureWebHostDefaults(webBuilder =>
            {

webBuilder.UseStartup<Startup>();
            })
            .ConfigureLogging(logging =>
            {
                logging.ClearProviders();

logging.SetMinimumLevel(LogLevel.Trace);
            });
}
```

3. Configure NLog in the `nlog.config` file:

```xml
Copy
<?xml version="1.0" encoding="utf-8" ?>
<nlog              xmlns="http://www.nlog-
project.org/schemas/NLog.xsd"
xmlns:xsi="http://www.w3.org/2001/XMLSche
ma-instance">
  <targets>
    <target name="logfile" xsi:type="File"
fileName="logs\\log.txt"
layout="${longdate}   ${level}   ${message}
${exception}" />
    <target              name="logconsole"
xsi:type="Console"     layout="${longdate}
${level} ${message} ${exception}" />
  </targets>
  <rules>
    <logger     name="*"     minlevel="Info"
writeTo="logfile,logconsole" />
  </rules>
</nlog>
```

- **Explanation**: NLog is configured with XML settings in the `nlog.config` file. It can write logs to multiple targets such as files and consoles.

3. Application Insights

Application Insights is a cloud-based monitoring solution by Microsoft, part of the **Azure Monitor** suite. It provides real-time application performance monitoring, error tracking, and powerful analytics for .NET applications.

Setting Up Application Insights:

1. Install the Application Insights SDK:

```bash
Copy
dotnet                add                package
Microsoft.ApplicationInsights.AspNetCore
```

2. Configure Application Insights in your `Startup.cs`:

```csharp
Copy
public                                    void
ConfigureServices(IServiceCollection
services)
{

services.AddApplicationInsightsTelemetry(
Configuration["ApplicationInsights:Instru
mentationKey"]);
}
```

3. Track custom events and exceptions:

```csharp
Copy
var      telemetryClient      =       new
TelemetryClient();
telemetryClient.TrackEvent("PaymentProces
singStarted");

try
{
    // Payment processing logic
}
catch (Exception ex)
{
    telemetryClient.TrackException(ex);
}
```

- **Explanation**: Application Insights provides detailed telemetry data on application performance, usage, and exceptions. It can be configured via the `InstrumentationKey` from the Azure portal, and

253

custom events can be tracked using the `TelemetryClient`.

Real-World Example: Implementing Logging in a Payment Processing System

In this example, we will implement **Serilog** for logging in a **payment processing system**. The system will log various events such as payment start, success, failure, and exceptions.

Step 1: Create the Payment Processing Service

```csharp
Copy
public class PaymentService
{
    private readonly ILogger<PaymentService> _logger;

    public PaymentService(ILogger<PaymentService> logger)
    {
        _logger = logger;
    }

    public void ProcessPayment(int userId, decimal amount)
    {
        try
        {
            _logger.LogInformation("Starting payment processing for UserId: {UserId}, Amount: {Amount}", userId, amount);

            // Simulate payment processing logic
            if (amount <= 0)
            {
```

```
                throw                   new
InvalidOperationException("Amount   must    be
greater than zero");
            }

        // Simulate successful payment
        _logger.LogInformation("Payment
successful   for   UserId:   {UserId},   Amount:
{Amount}", userId, amount);
    }
    catch (Exception ex)
    {
        _logger.LogError(ex,           "Error
processing payment for UserId: {UserId}, Amount:
{Amount}", userId, amount);
    }
  }
}
```

- **Explanation**: This service logs information when starting payment processing, successful payments, and errors.

Step 2: Configure Logging in `Program.cs`

```csharp
Copy
using Microsoft.Extensions.Hosting;
using Microsoft.Extensions.Logging;
using Serilog;

public class Program
{
    public static void Main(string[] args)
    {
        Log.Logger = new LoggerConfiguration()
            .WriteTo.Console()

.WriteTo.File("logs\\payment_processing_log.txt
", rollingInterval: RollingInterval.Day)
            .CreateLogger();

        try
        {
```

```
        Log.Information("Starting      payment
processing application...");

CreateHostBuilder(args).Build().Run();
        }
        catch (Exception ex)
        {
            Log.Fatal(ex, "Application failed to
start");
        }
        finally
        {
            Log.CloseAndFlush();
        }
    }

    public          static          IHostBuilder
CreateHostBuilder(string[] args) =>
        Host.CreateDefaultBuilder(args)
            .ConfigureLogging(logging =>
            {
                logging.ClearProviders();
                logging.AddSerilog();
            })
            .ConfigureServices((hostContext,
services) =>
            {

services.AddSingleton<PaymentService>();
            });
}
```

- **Explanation**: In the `Program.cs`, we set up **Serilog** to log to both the console and a file, ensuring logs are captured for both production and troubleshooting scenarios.

Step 3: Using the Payment Service

In the application, we call the `ProcessPayment` method to simulate processing a payment:

256

```csharp
Copy
public class PaymentProcessingApp
{
    private        readonly        PaymentService
_paymentService;

    public    PaymentProcessingApp(PaymentService
paymentService)
    {
        _paymentService = paymentService;
    }

    public void Run()
    {
        _paymentService.ProcessPayment(1, 100m);
        _paymentService.ProcessPayment(2, -5m);
// Will log an error
    }
}
```

- **Explanation**: The PaymentProcessingApp simulates the payment processing workflow, calling the ProcessPayment method and generating both successful and failed payment logs.

Best Practices for Monitoring and Logging

1. **Log Levels**: Use appropriate log levels (Information, Warning, Error, Critical) to differentiate between the severity of events.
2. **Structured Logging**: Use structured logging (e.g., Serilog) to log events in a consistent format, making it easier to query and analyze logs.
3. **Centralized Logging**: Store logs in a central location (e.g., ELK Stack, Azure Monitor) for easy access, search, and analysis.

4. **Monitor Key Metrics**: Continuously monitor application performance, health, and key business metrics to detect issues early.
5. **Alerting**: Set up automated alerts based on predefined thresholds (e.g., failed payment attempts, high latency) to notify developers or operations teams of potential issues.
6. **Security and Compliance**: Ensure sensitive information (e.g., credit card numbers, passwords) is never logged. Mask or redact sensitive data as needed.

This chapter covered the importance of **monitoring and logging** for enterprise applications, and how to implement logging using **Serilog**, **NLog**, and **Application Insights**. We provided a real-world example of **logging in a payment processing system**.

CHAPTER TWENTYSIX

Optimizing Performance in C# Applications

Profiling and Performance Tuning

Performance optimization is a critical aspect of building scalable and efficient applications. Profiling helps you identify bottlenecks, memory leaks, or inefficient code, while performance tuning focuses on resolving those issues to ensure the application performs well under different loads.

1. Profiling Tools in C#

Profiling involves monitoring various aspects of an application to understand how it behaves in terms of CPU, memory, and I/O usage. Profiling tools can give you insights into where your application is spending time, which methods are consuming excessive resources, and how to optimize them.

- **Visual Studio Profiler**: Visual Studio provides a built-in performance profiler that can track CPU usage, memory allocation, and more. It helps you understand which parts of your application are the most resource-intensive.
    - **How to use**:
        1. Open your project in Visual Studio.
        2. Go to **Debug** > **Performance Profiler**.

3. Start the profiling session, and Visual Studio will display data on CPU usage, memory, and network calls.

- **dotTrace (JetBrains)**: dotTrace is a powerful tool for .NET profiling, capable of measuring the performance of applications and identifying hotspots where the code spends too much time.
- **BenchmarkDotNet**: This library is perfect for benchmarking individual methods or classes. It can be used to measure execution time, memory usage, and performance under different scenarios.

Example: A simple benchmarking example using **BenchmarkDotNet**:

```csharp
Copy
using BenchmarkDotNet.Attributes;
using BenchmarkDotNet.Running;

public class MyBenchmark
{
    [Benchmark]
    public void TestMethod1()
    {
        // Some code to benchmark
    }

    [Benchmark]
    public void TestMethod2()
    {
        // Some other code to benchmark
    }

    public static void Main(string[] args)
    {
        var summary = BenchmarkRunner.Run<MyBenchmark>();
    }
}
```

2. Performance Tuning

Once you've identified the performance bottlenecks, the next step is tuning those parts of the application for better performance. Here are some common strategies:

- **Avoiding Unnecessary Object Creation**: Objects should be reused wherever possible. For instance, avoid repeatedly creating objects inside loops or frequently called methods.
- **Optimizing Loops**: Ensure that loops run efficiently, and try to minimize the number of iterations, especially in large datasets.
- **Using Efficient Data Structures**: Using the right data structure can significantly impact performance. For example, prefer `Dictionary<TKey, TValue>` for lookups instead of `List<T>` when you need fast lookups.
- **Avoiding Blocking Operations**: Synchronous operations can block the application, causing delays. Use `async/await` for I/O-bound tasks like network calls or file access to avoid blocking the main thread.

Memory Management and Garbage Collection

Memory management in C# is handled by the **.NET garbage collector (GC)**, which automatically reclaims memory used by objects that are no longer referenced. However, developers must be aware of how memory is used and managed to avoid performance degradation caused by inefficient memory allocation or GC pressure.

1. Garbage Collection in .NET

The **garbage collector** in .NET works in the background, collecting and cleaning up objects that are no longer in use. It uses a generational approach, categorizing objects into different generations:

- **Generation 0**: Short-lived objects. The GC collects these objects frequently.
- **Generation 1**: Objects that have survived at least one GC cycle.
- **Generation 2**: Long-lived objects, typically the objects that live throughout the application's lifetime (e.g., static objects, large collections).

When the GC runs, it performs the following:

1. **Marking**: The GC marks all objects that are still referenced.
2. **Sweeping**: It removes unreferenced objects and reclaims their memory.
3. **Compacting**: It compacts the memory to reduce fragmentation.

2. Managing Memory Usage

- **Minimize Memory Allocations**: Allocating memory frequently (especially in loops) puts pressure on the garbage collector. Reuse objects where possible, and try to use value types (structs) instead of reference types (classes) for small data structures that don't need to be shared.
- **Dispose of Unmanaged Resources**: For unmanaged resources (like file handles, database connections), use `Dispose` or `using` statements to ensure resources

are released immediately instead of waiting for garbage collection.

Example:

```csharp
Copy
using (var fileStream = new FileStream("file.txt", FileMode.Open))
{
    // Work with fileStream
} // fileStream.Dispose() is called automatically
```

- **Avoid Large Object Heap (LOH) Fragmentation**: Large objects (greater than 85,000 bytes) are allocated on the LOH. These objects are not compacted by the GC and can lead to fragmentation. Use smaller objects and arrays, or employ object pooling to avoid frequent allocations on the LOH.

Real-World Example: Optimizing a Large-Scale Data Processing Application

In this example, we will optimize a **large-scale data processing application** that processes a large number of records (e.g., transactions, user data, logs).

Step 1: Initial Application Design

Let's assume the application reads data from a file, processes it, and writes results to a database. The basic flow is:

1. **Read data from a file** (e.g., CSV or JSON).

2. **Process data**: For example, filtering, transformations, or aggregations.
3. **Write results to the database**.

Step 2: Profiling the Application

Start by profiling the application using tools like **Visual Studio Profiler** or **BenchmarkDotNet** to identify bottlenecks in CPU usage, memory allocation, and disk I/O. After profiling, you might find issues such as:

- **Excessive memory allocations**: The application creates too many objects, which leads to frequent garbage collection.
- **Inefficient disk I/O**: Reading large files or making many database writes.

Step 3: Implementing Optimizations

1. **Optimizing Memory Usage**:
   o Reuse objects in memory instead of creating new ones repeatedly.
   o Use `Span<T>` or `Memory<T>` for processing large arrays or buffers without allocating additional memory.
   o Avoid unnecessary allocations, especially inside loops, to reduce the pressure on the garbage collector.

Example: Using `Span<T>` for efficient memory access:

```csharp
Copy
public void ProcessData(Span<int> data)
{
    foreach (var item in data)
```

```
    {
        // Process each item
    }
}
```

2. Optimizing Data Processing:

- o Use **parallel processing** to distribute the work across multiple threads. This can be done using `Parallel.For` or **async/await** for asynchronous processing.

Example: Processing data in parallel:

```csharp
Copy
var data = File.ReadAllLines("largeFile.csv");

Parallel.ForEach(data, line =>
{
    // Process each line in parallel
});
```

3. Optimizing Disk I/O:

- o Minimize disk I/O by reading large files in chunks and processing data in memory.
- o Use **buffered readers** and **batch processing** to reduce the number of read and write operations.

Example: Using `StreamReader` with buffered reading:

```csharp
Copy
using (var reader = new StreamReader("largeFile.csv"))
{
    while (!reader.EndOfStream)
    {
```

```
        var line = reader.ReadLine();
        // Process the line
    }
}
```

4. **Optimizing Database Writes**:
   o Batch database writes into groups instead of writing records one by one.
   o Use **bulk insert** techniques when writing large datasets to avoid multiple round trips to the database.

Example: Batch inserting data into the database:

```csharp
Copy
using (var dbContext = new MyDbContext())
{
    var         transactions    =         new
List<Transaction>();
    for (int i = 0; i < 1000; i++)
    {
        transactions.Add(new Transaction {
Amount = i });
    }


dbContext.Transactions.AddRange(transacti
ons);
    dbContext.SaveChanges();    //     Bulk
insert
}
```

Step 4: Re-Profiling and Validation

After implementing optimizations, re-profile the application to ensure that the changes have improved performance. Validate the memory usage, processing time, and disk I/O. Monitor the application in a real-world environment to ensure it performs well under load.

Best Practices for Optimizing C# Applications

1. **Profile Early and Often**: Use profiling tools regularly to identify performance bottlenecks early in the development process.
2. **Use Asynchronous Programming**: For I/O-bound operations (e.g., file reading, database access), use asynchronous programming (`async`/`await`) to avoid blocking threads.
3. **Avoid Unnecessary Memory Allocations**: Be mindful of memory allocations, especially in high-performance applications or those that process large datasets.
4. **Leverage Parallelism**: Use parallel processing where applicable to make better use of multi-core CPUs, but be cautious of race conditions and thread safety.
5. **Use Efficient Algorithms and Data Structures**: Ensure that you are using the most efficient algorithms and data structures for your problem.
6. **Optimize Disk I/O**: Minimize disk read and write operations, and use buffered and batched operations to improve performance.

This chapter discussed **profiling, performance tuning**, and **memory management** in C# applications. We explored how to optimize a **large-scale data processing application** by reducing memory allocations, improving disk I/O, and parallelizing data processing.

CHAPTER SEVEN

Preparing for the Future: Modern C# Features and Practices

Exploring Latest Features of C#

The **C# language** continues to evolve with new features that make it more powerful, expressive, and developer-friendly. In recent years, several significant improvements have been introduced, particularly in C# 7, 8, 9, 10, and beyond. These features are designed to make development more efficient, improve performance, and enhance the readability and maintainability of code.

1. Record Types (C# 9)

Introduced in **C# 9**, **record types** provide a succinct syntax for defining immutable data objects. Records are ideal for representing data that should not change after creation, such as value objects or DTOs (data transfer objects).

Example:

```csharp
Copy
public record Person(string FirstName, string
LastName);
```

- **Explanation**: The `record` keyword defines an immutable object with built-in value equality, meaning two records with the same data are considered equal.

2. Pattern Matching (C# 9 and 10)

Pattern matching has been improved in C# 9 and C# 10 to provide more powerful and expressive ways to work with data. This includes **switch expressions, property patterns, and relational patterns**.

Example: Using **switch expressions**:

```csharp
Copy
public string GetPersonType(object person) =>
person switch
{
    Person p when p.Age < 18 => "Minor",
    Person p when p.Age >= 18 && p.Age <= 65 =>
"Adult",
    Person p => "Senior",
    _ => "Unknown"
};
```

- **Explanation**: The `switch` expression simplifies the syntax and makes it more expressive, allowing you to match on complex conditions, including properties.

3. Init-only Properties (C# 9)

Init-only properties allow you to create immutable objects that can be set during object initialization but not after. This enhances object immutability in a more intuitive way than `readonly`.

Example:

```csharp
Copy
public class Person
{
```

269

```
public string FirstName { get; init; }
public string LastName { get; init; }
}
```

- **Explanation**: With the `init` accessor, properties can be set only during object initialization, improving immutability.

4. Nullable Reference Types (C# 8)

C# 8 introduced **nullable reference types** as a way to reduce null reference exceptions by making reference types either nullable or non-nullable. This feature helps developers explicitly declare which variables can or cannot be `null`.

Example:

```csharp
csharp
Copy
public string? GetPersonName(Person person)
{
    return person?.Name;
}
```

- **Explanation**: The `string?` syntax indicates that the `Name` property can be `null`, and the nullable operator (`?.`) helps avoid null reference exceptions.

5. Asynchronous Streams (C# 8)

Asynchronous streams allow you to asynchronously iterate over collections or data streams using `await foreach`. This is particularly useful when working with data from external sources like APIs or databases.

Example:

```csharp
Copy
public          async          IAsyncEnumerable<int>
GetNumbersAsync()
{
    for (int i = 0; i < 10; i++)
    {
        await Task.Delay(100); // Simulate async
work
        yield return i;
    }
}
```

- **Explanation**: The IAsyncEnumerable interface allows for asynchronous iteration, making it easier to work with large datasets or time-consuming operations without blocking the main thread.

6. Source Generators (C# 9 and 10)

Source generators are a powerful feature introduced in C# 9 that allows developers to generate additional source code during compilation. This can be particularly useful for tasks like code generation, serialization, or automatic implementation of interfaces.

Example:

```csharp
Copy
[Generator]
public        class        MySourceGenerator        :
ISourceGenerator
{
    public                                      void
Initialize(GeneratorInitializationContext
context) { }

    public                                      void
Execute(GeneratorExecutionContext context)
```

271

```
    {
        // Generate code dynamically based on the
context
    }
}
```

- **Explanation**: Source generators allow for code to be generated at compile-time, providing a way to automatically generate code based on specific patterns or templates.

7. Records with Positional and Non-Positional Members (C# 10)

C# 10 further enhanced **records**, allowing you to define positional and non-positional members for greater flexibility in defining immutable objects.

Example:

```csharp
Copy
public record Person(string FirstName, string
LastName)
{
    public int Age { get; init; }
}
```

- **Explanation**: With C# 10, you can define both positional and non-positional members in records, providing greater flexibility while keeping the benefits of immutability and value equality.

Best Practices for Long-Term Maintainability

Building applications that are maintainable and adaptable over time is essential, especially in enterprise applications where requirements change and the system must evolve.

Here are some best practices for ensuring long-term maintainability:

1. Code Simplicity and Clarity

- **Keep it simple**: Avoid complex, convoluted logic. Write code that is easy to read and understand.
- **Clear Naming Conventions**: Use descriptive and consistent names for variables, methods, and classes.

2. Modularization

- **Separation of Concerns (SoC)**: Break the application into smaller, well-defined modules or services that each handle a specific responsibility. This makes it easier to update, test, and debug.
- **Use Design Patterns**: Use well-known design patterns like **Factory, Strategy**, and **Observer** to solve common problems in a consistent and maintainable way.

3. Documentation

- **Code Comments**: Comment complex or non-obvious code sections to ensure future developers understand why certain decisions were made.
- **External Documentation**: Document APIs, services, and business logic in external documentation to help with onboarding and maintenance.

4. Version Control and Branching

- **Git and Branching**: Use **Git** for version control and **branching strategies** (e.g., feature branches, release branches) to isolate development work and facilitate collaboration.

- **Tagging Releases**: Tag versions in Git to mark stable points in the development process, making it easier to roll back if needed.

5. Automated Testing

- **Unit Testing**: Write automated unit tests for all critical code paths to catch regressions early.
- **Integration Testing**: Ensure that integrated components work together as expected.
- **End-to-End Testing**: Automate tests that simulate real user interactions to ensure the application works as a whole.

6. Code Reviews

- **Peer Reviews**: Encourage peer code reviews to identify potential issues, enforce coding standards, and share knowledge within the team.
- **Continuous Refactoring**: Refactor the code periodically to improve its structure, readability, and performance.

7. Continuous Integration and Delivery (CI/CD)

- **CI/CD Pipelines**: Automate the building, testing, and deployment of your code using CI/CD pipelines to ensure faster and more reliable releases.

Real-World Example: Upgrading a Legacy Application with Modern C# Features

Let's consider a **legacy accounting application** built using C# 6 or earlier. This application is large and difficult to maintain, and the goal is to upgrade it to utilize modern C#

features like **records, pattern matching, nullable reference types**, and **asynchronous streams**.

Step 1: Upgrade the Project to the Latest C# Version

Start by upgrading the project to the latest version of C# (e.g., C# 10). Update the **.NET Core SDK** or **.NET 5/6/7** and modify the project settings accordingly.

Step 2: Use Records for Immutable Data Objects

In the legacy code, data models might be implemented as mutable classes. You can replace them with **records** for better immutability.

Before (Legacy Code):

```csharp
Copy
public class Transaction
{
    public int Id { get; set; }
    public decimal Amount { get; set; }
    public string Description { get; set; }
}
```

After (Modern C# Code):

```csharp
Copy
public record Transaction(int Id, decimal Amount, string Description);
```

- **Explanation**: Replacing the class with a `record` automatically provides value-based equality and makes the object immutable, ensuring data integrity.

Step 3: Introduce Nullable Reference Types

Enable nullable reference types in the project to prevent null reference exceptions and enforce more predictable behavior.

```csharp
Copy
#nullable enable

public                                           string?
GetTransactionDescription(Transaction?
transaction)
{
    return transaction?.Description;
}
```

- **Explanation**: Enabling nullable reference types helps catch potential null dereferencing issues at compile-time, improving code safety.

Step 4: Refactor with Pattern Matching

Refactor conditional logic with **pattern matching** to simplify the code and make it more expressive.

Before (Legacy Code):

```csharp
Copy
if (transaction.Type == "Income")
{
    // Process income
}
else if (transaction.Type == "Expense")
{
    // Process expense
}
```

After (Modern C# Code):

276

```csharp
Copy
transaction.Type switch
{
    "Income" => ProcessIncome(transaction),
    "Expense" => ProcessExpense(transaction),
    _ => throw new ArgumentException("Invalid
transaction type")
};
```

- **Explanation**: The switch expression provides a cleaner and more expressive way to handle multiple conditions.

Step 5: Introduce Asynchronous Streams

For handling large datasets, introduce **asynchronous streams** to process records without blocking the main thread.

Before (Legacy Code):

```csharp
Copy
foreach (var transaction in transactions)
{
    ProcessTransaction(transaction);
}
```

After (Modern C# Code):

```csharp
Copy
public async IAsyncEnumerable<Transaction>
GetTransactionsAsync()
{
    foreach (var transaction in transactions)
    {
        await Task.Delay(100); // Simulate async
work
        yield return transaction;
```

277

```
    }
}
```

- **Explanation**: The `IAsyncEnumerable` interface allows for asynchronous iteration over large datasets, making it more scalable and responsive.

Chapter Closing

In this chapter, we explored **modern C# features** such as **records, pattern matching, nullable reference types**, and **asynchronous streams**. We also covered best practices for ensuring **long-term maintainability** and demonstrated how to upgrade a **legacy application** to leverage these features for better readability, performance, and safety. By embracing these modern features and practices, you can significantly improve the quality of your code and prepare it for future changes.

www.ingramcontent.com/pod-product-compliance
Lightning Source LLC
La Vergne TN
LVHW051437050326
832903LV00030BD/3132

* 9 7 9 8 3 0 8 4 7 3 3 4 3 *